HAPPY

FEARNE COTTON

HAPPY

FINDING JOY IN EVERY DAY
AND LETTING GO OF PERFECT

Text © Fearne Cotton 2017
The right of Fearne Cotton to be identified as the author of this
work has been asserted in accordance with the Copyright, Designs
and Patents Act 1988.

First published in Great Britain in 2017 by Orion Spring,
an imprint of the Orion Publishing Group Ltd
This edition published in 2017 by Orion Spring
Carmelite House
50 Victoria Embankment
London EC4Y 0DZ
An Hachette UK Company

5 7 9 10 8 6

A CIP catalogue record for this book is available from the British Library.

ISBN: 978-1-409-17507-0

Photography (with the exception of page 180): Liam Arthur
Design: Ben Gardiner
Illustrations on pages 25, 36, 49, 62, 69, 93, 94, 97, 110, 119, 126,
136, 192, 211, 243, 250, 256: Fearne Cotton
Practical page illustrations: Abi Hartshorne
Yoga illustrations: Emanuel Santos
Rainbow self-reflection symbol: Shutterstock
Chapter and all other illustrations: Jessica May Underwood
Props: Rebecca Newport
Recipe tester: Jordan Bourke
Food styling: Iona Blackshaw
The Big Apple Experiment™ (page 172) was first pioneered by Nikki Owen in 2009
Printed in Great Britain by Clays Ltd, St Ives plc

The Orion Publishing Group's policy is to use papers that are natural,
renewable and recyclable and made from wood grown in sustainable
forests. The logging and manufacturing processes are expected to
conform to the environmental regulations of the country of origin.

www.orionbooks.co.uk

ORION
SPRING

TO JESSE, REX, HONEY, ARTHUR AND LOLA,

FOR THE HAPPINESS

YOU BRING

A LITTLE NOTE

Happiness. I think we often assume it's just around the corner, in the hands of others, or only for a chosen category of people. The beautiful thing is, it's actually there for the taking, inside us all the time, bubbling away waiting to be embraced.

I began my own exploration into the nebulous subject of happiness because throughout my life I have had patches where I have felt quite the opposite of 'happy'. Moments where I have stumbled into a darker territory – happy's grey and spiky sister: depression.

I have always been interested in looking at the world from various angles and exploring different emotions and their boundaries, but perhaps, previously, in a naive and reckless way. I wanted excitement; I wanted the rollercoaster; and I wanted it all quick. I remember writing in an old diary that I was 'prepared to experience it all'. I sprinted into joy without care or fear, and climbed as high as I could to get to it. Inevitably I would end up falling off a cliff edge on the other side to compensate for such highs, but I would quickly dust myself down and run at the next exciting hill. I admire my younger self for having such optimism and so little regard for anything negative that came my way but, my god, it was tiring.

I, like many people out there, assumed that once I had achieved certain accolades, climbed up the career ladder and felt love from those around me, I would feel 'happy'. Yes, there was happiness along the way, but my fast-paced, incautious way of living also led me to get hurt, feel empty at times and to live from my head rather than my heart.

Depression. Many of you will have experienced it or know someone who has. Maybe some of you have an inkling that you have dipped a toe into its murky waters, but have never really talked about it. It's an incredibly private experience but one that it's always better to share. I've never talked publicly about my own brush with depression before, as I feared it would make it bigger than it was, or that others would think I was being over-dramatic or attention-seeking. But now I think it's time for me to share my experiences, as being honest with myself, and others, can only be a good thing and in turn might help others, too.

Within these pages you'll hear me talk about what depression feels like for me, but you'll also find lots of happiness. Each of us has our own perspective on what it represents and how it feels. Wherever you currently are on the happiness spectrum – whether you're feeling down, okay or wonderful – I hope you can use this book to slow down, reflect and really engage with what those feelings are. For me, happiness and balance are about an open mind, an open heart and discipline. Nowadays, I like the simple things. Just give me fresh air, my kids' laughter, a paintbrush, people to cook for, a clear sky and plenty of sleep: these are my new cravings. I still get to feel excited and rocket-man high about things, but I know what will really deliver that balance and bliss that I have always craved. It's inevitable that we will all trudge through tough times, have to say goodbye to loved ones, beat ourselves up about things and make mistakes. Acceptance of this is key, as is the knowledge that 'happiness' is not a far-off destination that lives somewhere outside of YOU.

I've learned to get to grips with this, having spent so many years running far away from myself in search of it. I watched the sunset in many countries, climbed mountains, partied until the birds sang and did jobs that seemed so much bigger than me. I feel so lucky to have experienced these moments in my life, and fun and joy were definitely woven throughout them, but they weren't teleporting me to the island of happiness like I had hoped. Depression made me step back, slow down and realise this in a rather harsh and dev-astating way. Although painful to recall and write about now, I'm glad. I'm sort of grateful that I had this turning point. These days, I'm still prone to this darkness, so I have to be mindful about how I deal with everything around me.

Over time, I've learned a few simple things to help keep me in my version of 'happy'. These will be different for each of us, but I feel grateful for my own little list as it allows me to navigate back onto a smoother path when I find myself shunted off it. For example, painting ignites my inner dreamer as I put what's in my head onto a canvas; cooking gives me a creative outlet that acts like meditation.

These are some of the tools that together make a huge difference to my life and outlook. This book will combine these elements and more to help quieten your mind – through little exercises and visualisations – and hopefully drench you in relaxation and calm. I believe writing things down can be a very powerful tool to grab hold of; one that has helped me over the years and continues to help me make sense of the chaos in my head and digest thoughts, fears and dreams. Many of the exercises in the book involve just that, and I really hope this tool can be helpful to you, too.

This book will share ways to release what's going on inside your head and keep you trekking towards the good stuff. The simple stuff. The stuff that's going to really hit up that happiness on a deep and nourishing level. Whether you dip into these pages every now and then when you feel the need, or use the book's exercises for some daily positivity, I hope it brings you much relief, joy and calm.

Amen to the pen.

HAPPY *Not*

I want to begin here because it's ground zero: it explains why the subject of happiness is so important to me, and I hope it speaks to those of you who are struggling to find happiness right now.

This is the chapter I've been most fearful of writing, as delving back into this period of my life – that I can quite confidently describe as 'the dark patch' – makes me physically recoil. When I think of this time, my chest feels heavy and my throat tightens so it's hard to breathe. I have wanted to block it out and pretend it didn't happen, which isn't conducive to accepting and making peace with it. As you'll see when you read on, I think acceptance is a big part of awakening that inner happiness. So that's what I'll continue to strive for every day. I don't want this dark patch to be part of my story, but it is, so I will try to make friends with 'acceptance' and keep on trucking.

MY WALTZ WITH
THE DARKNESS

Depression. The big D. Not a word I say out loud a lot. If I ignored that period of my life and didn't breathe life into it with words, then maybe it would just go away; dissipate into dust that would float off into the ether. But pretending a certain part of your story didn't occur will only make it worse when something else in life reminds you unexpectedly of that time. You suddenly have to deal with all the emotional backlash without any warning or preparation. Making peace with your own backstory, and accepting that not all of it is good, is vital. Then, if you are dragged back into a memory or feeling from the past, your reaction will come from a calm place where you know you can cope.

I'm not quite there yet, and that's okay. I'm in no rush as I am confident that I'm headed in the right direction no matter what speed I travel at. Maybe that's also one reason I'm writing this book. It's certainly one of the reasons I've decided to be honest about this part of my life. Writing down the truth may breathe life into the subject, which is terrifying, but it also allows me to understand it a lot more and not keep it all locked away like some gruesome, eager monster.

Being honest isn't always easy, as you are instantly opening yourself up to judgement. It requires a certain amount of guts and, sometimes in life, that feels like a big effort; another reason why, until now, I haven't talked about any of this. I haven't had the energy to witness and process the array of possible reactions.

But being honest also allows me to share my story, which I hope will help some of you reading this and stop the subject of depression being such a taboo. Maybe you have experienced a similar situation in your life. Maybe you will simply enjoy jotting down your own notes and ideas on these pages. Maybe my words will help you retrieve your own, and in turn help you find the courage to share your own experience with others. That would feel like a really special transaction.

THE CLOUD

Depression has many faces and can creep in at any speed. For some it's hereditary and something they may have been warned about from a young age. My mother and grandmother both suffered with it to varying degrees, so I always knew how it could affect the joys of life. Sometimes depression will swamp your life after an incident that leaves you feeling lost or out of control; sometimes maybe there's just no rhyme or reason. Mine was a whirlwind of all of these and that frenetic concoction meant it came in thick and fast.

I wasn't even sure what I was going through at the time – all I knew was that I was walking through this thick mud that was making every step exhausting and debilitating. It can be tricky to know when you've crossed the line from feeling a bit blue to depression. Throughout my twenties, my blue moments were mostly linked to what every other twenty-something would be going through: break-ups, heartache, lack of confidence and generally feeling a bit lost. I had no previous reference point to gauge whether I had dipped my toe into depression's treacle, or if I was merely feeling a bit down. In the end it was the length of time I felt stuck that rang alarm bells, and the fact I felt there was no hope of finding a way out.

Everyone's physical and mental version of depression will differ but, for me, it was a cloud. A dark, ominous mountain of a cloud that made my heart sink when I looked at it. My inner light that used to shine so brightly had dimmed to being barely visible. The optimistic sunshine in my eyes had been replaced by a heaviness and my skin matched the drab grey of the giant cloud. I always used to look forward to what lay ahead, even something as simple as my morning coffee, but during this period nothing seemed hopeful.

It was hard to leave the house during this time but I was still needed at work on a daily basis. Due to the nature of my job I would put on a fake smile, walk out of the door, go into robot mode and get through what was needed. Most of the time it was like an out-of-body experience. Someone else was pushing the buttons and making things happen, as I certainly wasn't capable of it. When my work was done, I could lift off the mask and privately fall apart. The tears would flow, followed by a feeling of complete numbness.

NUMB

Whenever I experienced this numb feeling I knew I was trapped. Have you ever noticed that the natural flow of life is to keep moving? We are always travelling from one experience and emotion to the next. We cannot sustain pure happiness or sorrow for huge lengths of time without the tiniest interval of something else. So the numbness alerted me to the fact that I was stuck, and stuck in a really shitty place, imprisoned in this thick fog with no way out. It was like a bland and blank page of nothingness. Even my natural aptitude for gathering happiness from nostalgia was sucked dry. Everything felt quite dead, drained and shell-like. The only thing that would awaken me from this state was the shocking

HELLO TO . . . MUM

Writing this book has allowed a dialogue to open up between me and my mum. We have always been very close but for some reason hadn't delved into an honest discussion about depression before. This book made me brave a chat about it that I had been subconsciously putting off, and knowing that depression has woven its way through generations of my family has allowed me to unpick my own experiences with more clarity and understanding. Mum's honesty has been a huge help. Over to her . . .

" I think it was Churchill who called his depression 'the black dog'. I would call mine 'the black pit'. This is what it feels like: being in a dark hole unable to pull yourself out of it. It's not just sadness, it's more than that. There is the feeling of worthlessness, the feeling of 'what's the point?', being unable to concentrate, negative thoughts spinning out of control, etc. My mother had depression and anxiety and whether this is passed on through the generations, I don't know. But I do know that my triggers include reading too much negative news – we hear bad news from all over the world instantly and I suppose you feel bombarded and powerless to help; the media seem to revel in reporting more bad stuff than good stuff. I spiral downwards when I see man's inhumanity to man. I spiral downwards when I see how cruel humans are to defenseless animals – I support many animal charities and some of the stories I read are heartbreaking. I spiral downwards when I see how our planet is being exploited – it could all be so different. My defence mechanism is to shut myself off from it occasionally and give my brain a rest. I don't think we are designed to know and cope with what is happening all over the world all the time. I try to be kind to myself, get into nature, walk, sleep, eat well and keep life as simple as I can. Trying to help others (humans and animals) also lifts me. I suppose I say to myself: 'You have been here before, it will pass . . . tomorrow is another day.' "

feeling of panic. My heartbeat would quicken and bile would rush to my throat. It was like waking up from a night's sleep to find yourself running a marathon. It was disorientating and scary.

WHAT DOES BLACK FEEL LIKE?

We've all felt BLUE at some point. It's inevitable. It could start from a tiny seed of worry or sorrow and snowball into a vast area of your life. It could be your go-to emotion as it feels safe and comforting. How could anyone hurt you if you're already down? How could it get any worse? It's far from the best comfort zone to slip into, as I have learned many a time. You will only attract more of that energy into this space as that's the message you're giving off to others – and if susceptible, it could lead you into feeling BLACK.

In my experience, feeling 'black' has a close alliance with fear. Not the type of fear that makes you alert and on guard, but the sort that can eradicate hope in one gulp. It swallows it up and spits out the remains, your dreams and hopes, in tatters.

The fear clingfilms your body and suffocates any confidence you had in yourself. This fear has a partner in crime, a shouty voice booming: 'You're ridiculous for believing you could fulfil your dreams! How selfish and arrogant of you.'

This lethal combination extracts all the innocence from your dreaming and stops you in your tracks. It has the power to draw up safely filed-away memories that make you flinch to retrieve. Memories you had filed under 'horrific', 'embarrassing', 'full of shame'. It draws them up, projects them onto the forefront of your mind and illuminates them on a cinema-sized screen. This fear makes you believe you are defined by these moments and won't let you forgive yourself for mistakes and dark times.

This black feeling is drenched in indifference and lethargy but has an inner electric edge that won't let you relax. You're asleep in body, but wired in mind: a toxic partnership that has no balance at all. You're down the rabbit hole with no instructions on how to get out or find the light again.

TALK. TALK. TALK.

I was too drenched in this circle of sorrow and panic to notice what was really going on. A dear friend of mine suggested, quite insistently, that I see a doctor. Realising others could see something wasn't right, I silently got in her car and met with the doctor who instantly saw what was up.

HELLO TO . . . MIND

I have been aware of Mind's fantastic work for a long time and visited their head office a few years back. They are a fount of knowledge on mental health and a sturdy support network for many. I'm very grateful for their encouragement with my book and for this little chat I had with Paul Farmer, the CEO.

F: If someone out there thinks they are experiencing depression what should they be looking out for? What signs might point to a mental health issue?

P: Well, many of us will feel down from time to time, but you may notice at some stage in your life that you've actually been feeling low for a couple of weeks or more, or that the low feeling returns over and over again, which could mean that you're potentially experiencing depression.

Symptoms of mental health problems vary from person to person, but there are some common symptoms of depression to look out for. Someone might feel restless, numb or helpless, lose interest in sex, sleep too much or too little, and gain no pleasure from things they used to enjoy. Those experiencing depression can often become disconnected from other people, so may find themselves withdrawing from contact with friends or family. At its most severe, someone may feel like there's no point in the future, or even – in some cases – think about suicide; so it's really important to recognise any symptoms as early as possible and seek out help to try to avoid this.

F: What is the first thing they should do if they want help?

P: Seeking help is absolutely one of the most important things to do if you feel like you're experiencing a mental health problem. The first step is to speak to someone – it could be a friend or family member you trust, or speaking to your GP who can talk you through the support that's available. We know that talking to your GP might seem a little daunting for some – an extra thing that you have to worry about – so Mind have produced a guide on how to speak to your GP about your mental health, which you can find on the Mind website **mind.org.uk/findthewords.**

F: How important is it to share your worries and fears with someone?

P: It's really important to talk to the people close to you about how you're feeling as having support systems in place, like a friend or family member to talk to, can be a huge help.

If you've talked through your mental health problems with someone in the past, it also makes it easier for people to pick up on changes in your behaviour and give you support should you need it again.

Talking about your worries, fears, or mental health is also the most powerful tool in breaking down the stigma that sometimes still surrounds mental health. Everyone has mental health, so it's important for us to make sure that problems aren't seen as anything to be ashamed of. At Mind, we strongly believe that this generation can be more open about mental health problems than any generation before.

F: What do you as a charity offer up to people who feel they might be going through a mental health issue?

P: Put simply, Mind provides both advice and support to empower anyone experiencing a mental health problem. As a charity we believe everyone experiencing a mental health problem should get both support and respect, and therefore we offer a variety of services to people who feel they might be going through a mental health issue.

There is the Mind Infoline (0300 123 3393), which provides information on a range of topics, including types of mental health problems, where to get help, medication and alternative treatments. Mind also has its network of over 140 Local Minds, each offering unique services tailored to the needs of their community. Services include talking therapies, peer support, advocacy, crisis care, employment and housing support – so there should be something on offer to suit everyone's individual situation and preference.

Mind also produces information booklets and runs an online forum for people to discuss their problems and possible solutions with others who are going through similar experiences called Elefriends (elefriends.org.uk).

We'd encourage everyone to look on our website (mind.org.uk) if you want to find out more as it really does have a vast amount of information and resources on it – including an A–Z of mental health and blog posts and podcasts where you can listen to people describing their own experiences of different mental health problems.

F: Why do you think some choose to shut off and not speak up when they're struggling?

P: The fear of being judged or isolated. The way that some people potentially think and act about mental health can silence people at a time when they need support the most. It's important that everyone feels able to talk about their mental health problems without fearing the attitudes of others.

There are things we can do as a society though to help change this. Mind run a joint campaign with Rethink Mental Illness called 'Time to Change' that specifically works towards changing outlooks and behaviours, and have subsequently encouraged 95,000 individuals and organisations to pledge to end mental health stigma.

If someone you know doesn't seem their normal selves and you're concerned about them, for example if they have started avoiding social contact, it's best to ask them how they're feeling. It takes a lot for someone to say "I need help", but it doesn't hurt to raise the subject yourself. Sometimes you don't have to explicitly talk about mental health to find out how they're doing – it can be as simple as texting them to let them know you're thinking of them, inviting them out for coffee or dinner or going for a walk. It can often be the little things that actually make a big difference to someone's mental health.

Mind is a mental health charity that aims to help anyone experiencing a mental health problem.
Website: mind.org.uk. Info line: 0300 123 3393 (open 9am to 6pm, Monday to Friday – except for bank holidays). Email: info@mind.org. uk. To support the charity, visit mind.org.uk/get-involved.

It was almost a relief to give it a name – perhaps it wasn't all me and my thoughts; perhaps depression chose me and I had little choice in the matter. That made things a tiny weeny bit easier. Giving it a name made it feel like I was on loan to depression and I could now do whatever possible to get back to feeling like myself again.

I am very lucky that I love communicating and always have done but weirdly, at this point, the matter at hand felt too heavy to express. Deep down I knew it would help ease the pain and shame of it all so eventually I braved it and opened up about what I had been experiencing. A few very special people in my life provided an incredible ear and helped me feel like there would be a time when all of this would pass. Their belief in me and support made me feel safe and that's a great start.

My advice would be to pick carefully who you choose to talk to. Go with your gut. I made the mistake at one point of choosing someone whose strength of character and confidence seemed reassuring, but the person in question instantly shut down a dialogue that I thought might be a way out for me. I felt foolish for a long time, but I realise now that maybe I shouldn't have burdened someone I didn't have a long-standing relationship with. Save the big chats and honest words for people who you know have you in their hearts full-time. Whether that be to a friend who can talk to you, or a professional who can offer help. Speak up and be honest. Let them in and let them help you. Talking to people, the right people, is a gift, and one to be used when you know you need it. It's integral to climbing this steep and treacherous mountain.

FIND YOUR TOOLS

For me, medication was advised as the next appropriate tool to help lift me out of the pit I had sunk into. I didn't stay on medication for long, but for the short time I was taking it I managed to lift my head high enough to see the light again. The numbness was still there but I could sense happiness on a small scale, and smile and mean it. Once you get started, you can then find the momentum to roll, and that's exactly what I did.

Everyone will have a different opinion on how to live with depression and may have their own personal preferences on how to deal with it. For me, medication was a last resort and one I used only momentarily, but I'm thankful for the gear change the medicine provided so I could then look with clarity for other options for the long term. Whatever feels right to you is the best way. Follow your gut.

Finding other methods to deal with what I feared in life, and how

I perceived my own story, was now my new mission. First, I looked around at my life and worked out what needed to go. I had built up beliefs about myself, about others around me and about how the world worked that weren't conducive to a healthy mental state long-term. This needed to change. This switch-up took time and felt strange at first, but it has led me to a place where I feel I can put my time and energy into the things I really care about. Being surrounded by positive people and feel-good activities that make me feel alive is very important to prevent my mind from wandering into any shadowy territory.

I also learned to recognise ways of thinking that can lead me to feeling blue. I now try to place far less importance on what everyone else thinks and says around me and instead focus on what I believe to be the truth. Something I still have to work on relentlessly. Sometimes I feel defined by my own story, forgetting that I am the one writing it, and I can get swamped by wondering how I fit into it all. Rather than just sitting happy in the NOW and knowing I'm okay, I can lean more towards worrying about mistakes I've made in the past and things I could have done differently. I have to deal with these ways of thinking; I can't fight them, as they will only grow stronger. I have to replace them with new ways of viewing life.

Occasionally I'll still jump off the high-board into the blue, and from there I can see the darkness just across the water, but with my new ways of thinking in place it's much less likely that I'll be dragged under the current. Learning what your triggers and weaknesses are is important, as you can then try to avoid certain situations or thought processes that you know lead you down a dark and gloomy path.

ESCAPING THE BLACK

When you're in the black, it feels endless. *How will this giant cloud ever pass, and how will I not be affected by the memory of it?* That's where hard work and discipline comes into play. As soon as I remember, in a tiny chink of light, that everything has been okay before, and that I can experience happiness again, I can start to heave myself out. It takes one thought, one second, one moment or positive memory to act as a catalyst for the light to gradually seep in again. Shapes change, moods shift, lungs fill, feet shuffle and clouds start to part. Hope, joy, love and laughter: it's all for the taking once you get your head in the right space.

The next step is not running head on into another loaded emotion too quickly. Sprinting full pelt into excitement or drama could be just as damaging, so I try to remember to take it slowly and not numb the feeling of 'black' by covering it with another heightened emotion. I let it flow naturally, however long that might take, and use building blocks of things I love to help climb that slippery flight of stairs.

THERE'S ROOM FOR IT ALL

My friend, Gerad Kite, uses a wonderful theory of the 'Pendulum'. Gerad is an incredible acupuncturist who has studied Five Element acupuncture for over twenty years. This theory leads you to notice your own natural swing of emotions. Rather than swing with great force from one feeling to another, you can sit above it all, on the top of the Pendulum, and observe it unfolding. But neither should you try to stay in the middle of your pendulum and block out extreme emotions. We can all feel scared of getting too happy, as it's often sidelined by the fear of that moment or good thing ceasing to exist. Fall into good times feeling safe, but knowing of course that it will have a natural end. The same with the darker times. All this too shall pass. If, like me, 'blue' or 'black' is one of your go-to states, let it come and pass naturally. Don't get stuck in it for too long and don't feel desperate to block it out or numb it with other feelings. There's room for it all.

HELLO TO . . . GERAD

I have been working as a Five Element acupuncturist for almost thirty years and I am in the business of helping people find balance in their lives. When we swing out of balance, symptoms – friendly messengers – emerge to tell us we've lost our footing and that we are getting sick. Throughout my career, I have noticed that no matter the physical symptom a person brings into the room – unhappiness quickly follows too. From the perspective of Five Element acupuncture all symptoms are indicators that we have lost internal balance.

When I originally trained as a psychotherapist, I was introduced to a therapeutic tool called the 'Pendulum'. This simple but powerful image was given to help people find balance. Whenever we talk about finding balance we typically compare one state to another. 'Am I working too hard or am I being lazy?' 'Am I partying too much or is my life as dull as dishwater?' The other option on the table is the midpoint or the balancing point, i.e. working in moderation; leaving the party at 11pm to ensure a good night's sleep. But if we're honest, that sounds less appealing than the extremes of the pendulum swings.

But if we are to find real and lasting happiness in our lives we need to abandon our obsession with hunting the highs and resisting the lows and discover the hidden secrets of the 'calm'.

The 'calm' is the natural balancing point of the pendulum swing. This should be our natural state; the highs and lows of life are places we can visit – but never remain. When we start to suffer or feel unhappy it is because we are stuck in the highs or the lows or swinging madly between both. The humble middle ground is the path to contentment and peace. Focus your attention there and your mood and body will follow suit.

Summary

TALK.

If you slip into the blue or indeed the black, don't keep it in. Find someone you trust – friend or professional – and tell them about it.

FIND YOUR TOOLS.

Work out what facilitates unhappiness in your life and look at how you could eradicate any frameworks that allow it to creep in.

THERE'S ROOM FOR IT ALL.

Don't panic if you feel unhappy. Let it come and go. Remember: all this too shall pass.

NOTHING VENTURED, NOTHING GAINED

Before I crack on with my story and the little things that have helped – and continue to help – me on my quest for happiness, take a look inside yourself and really gather what's going on with you right now. Don't be afraid to be honest. Take stock of how you're feeling – only then can you understand where it is you want to go.

How are you feeling today?	terrible	bad	OK	good	great
How's your work-life balance?	terrible	bad	OK	good	great
How does the past feel to you?	terrible	bad	OK	good	great
How does the future feel to you?	terrible	bad	OK	good	great
How are you at putting your phone away?	terrible	bad	OK	good	great
How does your brain feel?	terrible	bad	OK	good	great
How are your stress levels?	terrible	bad	OK	good	great
What's the food you're eating like?	terrible	bad	OK	good	great
How's your health?	terrible	bad	OK	good	great
How's your exercise output?	terrible	bad	OK	good	great
How are you at being positive?	terrible	bad	OK	good	great
How are you at communicating?	terrible	bad	OK	good	great
How are you at being thankful?	terrible	bad	OK	good	great
How are things with your family?	terrible	bad	OK	good	great
How are your friendships?	terrible	bad	OK	good	great
How are your happiness levels, overall?	terrible	bad	OK	good	great

HAPPY *Balance*

For me, having a 'happy balance' is the cornerstone of contentment. Balance doesn't make us instantly think of beaming joy and elation, but to me HAPPINESS isn't that at all. It's not a saccharine sweet thumbs-up, it's a calm and considered, grounded peace.

Balance can be achieved by doing enough of what makes you tick. Life is full of responsibility and potential stress, so it's important we find a balance in it all.

I personally need to make sure I balance out being a mum, working, and quenching my creative thirst. I can then feel I'm giving my all to my children, husband, work and myself in equal amounts. In turn, I can enjoy it all, as I know there's a balance and system that works for me.

Your own balance will be different from mine. It's all about identifying YOUR balance and working towards it.

PERSEVERE

Finding balance isn't necessarily easy, and can be especially hard when you are faced with unexpected adversity. Like many people, I have experienced loss, bereavement, shock and trauma. Some of these experiences remain with me and it takes work to turn down the negative and focus on life's upsides, especially as trauma can feel like it's living in your every cell, attaching itself like a leech and refusing to loosen its grip. Everyone deals with this differently, but for me, creating balance in life is key. Allowing yourself time to stop and take stock is how you will heal and repair, then that grip will start to loosen and you'll be able to see the sunshine again.

I'm an all-or-nothing person. If I fall in love, I free-fall without a parachute. If I have a goal in sight, I become blind to much else of what lies around me. If I feel an emotion, it tends to be at the extreme end of the spectrum. So acquiring balance in my life doesn't necessarily come naturally to me. It's something I have to work at and be vigilant about.

But I reckon it's okay to not have cracked this one completely, as it takes time and requires a fundamental change in how you think about life. You almost have to rewrite what you thought you knew, and that's never going to be quick.

OUR INNER ALARM CLOCK

Sometimes I exhaust myself with the pressure I've put myself under, of trying to do so much at once and all to a certain standard. I constantly fret that I'm not doing enough, or that I'm getting complacent in areas. I feel extremely lucky as I love being a mum and I am insanely passionate about my job, so doing too much is usually fun. Writing this book, for instance, is making me buzz and burst with happiness, as I love having a goal and a project and writing honestly is proving to be cathartic. After a day with the kids, or on a shoot, I write, write, write until my eyes are blurry and my husband leads me to bed, where I will have a shorter-than-ideal night's sleep as our young children wake up early.

I like this way of life as I constantly remember 'you only live once'. I want to push myself, but inevitably I know that at some point the scales will begin to tip and my body or my mind will scream out for some calm, and that will be my inner alarm clock warning me to get the balance back.

In this day and age, it is very difficult to NOT burn out. There are so many opportunities out there and so much pressure to do everything possible. Maybe we want or need to work hard, or feel we should be working harder. Maybe we love socialising and try to squeeze this into an already overflowing calendar. Maybe we

Here is your **inner alarm clock**. Mark a cross where you feel you are at today. Particularly if you are in 'Stressed', close to the alarm bells, physically draw yourself away from there into the quarter you'd like to be in. What small change can you make in this moment to help you get there?

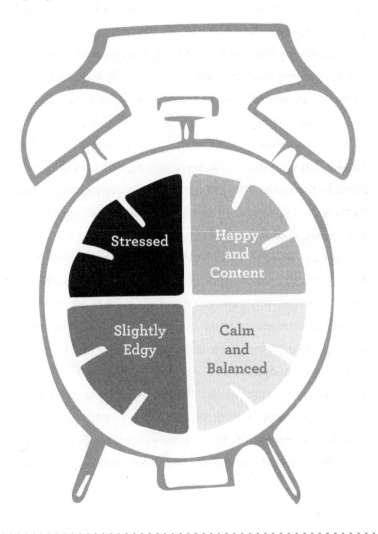

need to help others around us and forget to take a look at how we ourselves are coping. It always seems that there are simply not enough hours in the day, and we don't have the energy to do all we need or want.

'SHOULD DO' AND 'WANT TO'

Whenever I get into this exhausted mindset I try to distinguish between the things I feel I should be doing and the things I want to be doing. Usually even the dullest 'SHOULD DO' has an underlying element of 'WANT TO' when you bear in mind the goal you are trying to achieve. 'I SHOULD go to the gym' could mean 'I WANT to feel good', for example.If it's coming from a place where you know inner happiness lies and can be achieved at the end of it, then run with it. If the WANT is coming from a place of fear and low self-esteem, and is making you feel rubbish, then it's time to ditch that aim and work out what really makes you tick.

Getting balance in your life has to be a personal project. I really believe that you cannot compare your life with others. You must decide how to devote your own time and energy, and not be swayed by what others do. It has to feel good to you. You may have a colleague who works much harder than you. If it doesn't feel right to you to have that much time taken up by work, then don't try to match what your friend is doing. Work out your own needs and what makes you feel really good.

To give you my own example, I rarely go out socialising these days. That's because top of the ladder in terms of what makes me feel good are spending time with my kids and husband, and working. The next rung down is for friends and activities that fall into daytime hours. Going out at night, like I did in my twenties, has fallen off the priority ladder altogether. I haven't the energy for it. Or, should I say, I have CHOSEN not to give the energy I have to it. This may change again later in my life but for now it feels like the best way of preserving energy for my priorities.

I have made that choice, and very happily. Occasionally I'll get FOMO, but much less regularly these days as I get so much balance and enjoyment from the chosen activities of my day-to-day life. It's a challenge, but if you listen to your inner voice you'll know what you really want, so hopefully you can start saying goodbye to some SHOULDs.

WHAT DOES IMBALANCE
FEEL LIKE?

So you have your list of WANT TOs and they feel great. How are you supposed to know when you've reached the road sign that states TOO MUCH?

I think most people get out of balance because they have a fear of what might happen if they change their habits – or they don't realise how much damage a habit is doing to them. Some people are out of balance physically, as I myself was earlier in life. I ate on the run, didn't mind what fuel I ran on and let lack of sleep and little rest run my body down. Some people might over-eat or under-eat to feel in control, overlooking that the outcome won't lead to balance or happiness. Some people are imbalanced with their time, working too much or focusing on just one thing, and therefore missing out on something else they might enjoy.

If I feel my balance tip in life and my basket getting too full, I shriek and wail that it's all too much and I can't cope, as I'm sure we all do at times. I am learning to take a step back while remembering I have the power to change my situation and how I react to it all.

LISTEN TO YOUR GUT

All we can truly do is be aware of our own inner barometer (see the next page!). This will be different for everyone but it's essentially a case of listening to your gut and what you want to be doing with your time. It's so much easier said than done, but once you get more in tune with it, it gets easier and easier.

Growing up, I chased excitement and adventure and pushed everything else aside. I had little respect or regard for rest or peace, so stomped through situations with clompy shoes and my eyes closed. I would work until I lost sight of that fact that I had chosen to do so and would complain that I was too tired or overworked. I had chosen to live at that speed and hadn't created room for any other pace. Now I realise there is another way.

TAKING TIME TO STOP

What we all forget at times is self-preservation. When we forget to make sure we are doing okay, we can't then give our best to the people we care about. Finding time for this can sometimes seem impossible, but it is integral to achieving that much-needed balance in life.

Here is my own barometer of happiness. It's powerful to write down what makes you tick and how you can return to this, or at least try, when things get tough. You then have a constant gauge on where you are at happiness wise and know what to do and go back to if you're not feeling so great. Complete your own barometer on the next page.

Happy, content and balanced	Being with my family, feeling fit and healthy, eating well. The simple stuff.
Full of joy and energy	Eating lovely food. Laughter and friends. Having creative flow with art, cooking and music.
Feeling calm and at peace	Getting outside. Doing yoga and sleeping well.
Neutral and observant	Listening to others.
Low energy and jaded	Comparing myself to others. Listening to others' thoughts about me. Worrying about health.
Sad and down	Not getting my life/work balance right. Not spending enough time with my kids.
Depressed	Getting into situations where I dont feel I'm good enough. Listening to my demons and losing self-worth.

My husband and I have weird schedules and little routine which makes planning anything tricky, but we do try to have the odd date night where we'll get a babysitter. If we can't even manage this, we just try to make time to talk. To sit, without phones or screens, and just talk. It's always interesting to just chat and have fun rather than talk about who has washed the school uniforms and packed lunches. Every couple has good times and bad times but we feel it's important for us, and our kids, that we remain strong by making little moments like this count.

My husband regularly tells me to get off my laptop in the evenings when the kids are in bed and orders me to have a bath. My reply is always a stroppy: 'I haven't got time for a bath!' Okay, so I may have thirty emails to write and three birthday presents I need to buy online for family members, but maybe having a bath for thirty minutes to ground myself and stop my brain ticking will refresh me for all that lies ahead. Maybe I could find thirty minutes tomorrow to finish up emails when I've rested properly. Our days are short but there is usually some room for movement if you're willing to sacrifice a little of something else. Rest and stopping has to take a priority where it can. I'm reiterating this as I'm useless at it!

THE SECRET OF SLOWING DOWN

I know that when I get closely involved in a project I'm excited about, it's partly to do with the fact I love to feel busy and useful, but it's also to do with the fear of stopping. What if I truly stopped? How would I feel? Would my demons creep back up and shout in my face? Would I be able to handle what arises? My inner compass will always spin towards the route of exhaustion and boundary-pushing, but I now try to reprogramme my mindset to take a little time to stop, get centred and look around me. I tend to favour the kind of 'stopping' that allows me to trick my mind into thinking I'm still 'doing'. Yoga, painting, running or cooking – with these types of activities, my mind stops but a slight blissful ticking remains. This suits my over-active brain – and probably quells my underlying fear of truly letting go! Learning to slow down and stop once in a while is a tricky change to make, and you have to be prepared for where your mind might go once you've stopped trying to distract it with other things. For example, you may have memories or worries that you need to come to terms with. I think facing these things is a better option than battling on and covering your troubles by keeping busy.

FIVE TINY WAYS TO STOP.

We may feel like we have no time in the day, but these small changes in our lives can allow us to morph time to our own liking ...

1. **Take time when you eat.** Make sure you can sit and enjoy every mouthful of what is in front of you.

2. **Turn your phone off at night.** Choose a time that feels right for you and don't allow yourself to text or send emails past this moment. Mine usually goes off at 9pm and doesn't go back on until after breakfast the next day.

3. **Go and stand outside for five minutes come rain or shine.** Stepping outside of your usual environment for a short time will give you the head space you need to crack on with the rest of the day. It's like smoking without the smoking!

4. **Doodle.** Rather than scouring the internet after work or before bed, why not get back to basics – get a pen and paper and doodle away. You don't have to be any good at drawing, it's more the motion and focus needed that's great for your brain.

5. **Take a real look around you.** You can be in the busiest of environments but still feel you're in a calm place by just stopping and observing the scene. See others, listen to the sounds around you, feel the quality of air, sense the clothes on your skin, be aware of your breath leaving each nostril. Stopping without actually stopping just requires a bit of awareness.

HELLO TO . . . TOM

I have known Tom Fletcher for many years, but had no clue what was going on in his personal life until he opened up so eloquently in the 2012 McFly autobiog-raphy, Unsaid Things, about his bipolar disorder. I found this truly inspiring and courageous and have enjoyed many chats since with Tom on the subject. He knows his honest approach can help others, so he's always willing to share his thoughts and talk about how he views life since his diagnosis. I was intrigued to hear his thoughts on happiness when I began writing this book, so had a chat with him about how bipolar disorder affects his daily barometer of joy.

F: Hey Tom, how are you today?

T: I'm great. Really great. I'm on another level of tiredness right now because of the kids and work, but things are great.

F: Thanks so much for talking to me about, as you described it to me, your 'wonky brain'. It takes guts to be honest and show your vulnera-bilities. What made you first want to speak out about it all?

T: Well, I only realised that I wasn't the only one with this sort of 'wonky brain' by seeing someone else speak openly about it. I was having a par-ticularly tough time and by chance caught Stephen Fry's documentary about bipolar on TV [*The Secret Life of the Manic Depressive*, BBC One, 2006] and it was a really emotional moment, because it was like listening to someone describe my own life. That was the start of me discovering how my 'wonky brain' works.

When it came to writing the McFly autobiography we agreed that we would be completely open about everything, so it felt wrong to leave it out – I thought that if writing about my own experience could help just one person then that is surely worth it.

F: When did you first notice that something might not feel quite right with your mental health?

T: I think I experienced some sort of heightened emotions from a very young age, perhaps ten or eleven. I can trace regular patterns of highs and lows back to the start of McFly and that was in 2003, but when I think back to how I felt and reacted to situations at a younger age I think I can spot certain signs of it in my childhood.

F: You were diagnosed with bipolar. When you've hit one of those lows, what does depression feel like to you?

T: My diagnosis itself was actually quite a complicated experience. I went to different doctors, psychiatrists and psychologists, all with different opinions. Some with a more black-and-white 'you have bipolar' diagnosis, and others who were a little more vague. That in itself is confusing when you're going through a bad time and really need some answers, but I learnt a lot about myself during that process and eventually got the right treatment and help.

Back to your question though . . . the lows suck. They suck more than anything else I can think of. They made me the worst version of me that I can be in every way, but I think the weirdest part of my lows (and the hardest part to explain) isn't that there is no light at the end of the tunnel, but that you don't want there to be. It's like you're committed to being in this low and won't even look for the way out.

F: What does bipolar mean to you? How does it feel and how do you visualise it?

T: I guess the difficult thing I found with my bipolar is that I felt that it had become so much a part of who I am that I was scared about getting rid of it. I felt that the high points, the 'ups', made me extremely creative and full of positive energy that made anything seem possible. I was very worried about losing that. I guess I was associating any talent I might have with these 'ups' and was worried that, by starting to take medication to control the lows, I might lose my creativity.

F: How did this affect those around you?

T: When I told the guys in the band I think it was a big collective, 'Oh, that's what it is . . . so you're not just a dick'. Haha. I put them through a lot over the years during my down times and I know I was extremely difficult to live with and work with. They put up with a lot. Although no one put up with more than my wife, Gi. She would call it my 'period' when I was in one of my lows and that was long before we knew anything about depression or bipolar.

F: How do you feel on a daily basis now that you take medication?

T: I've actually stopped taking it now. I was taking it daily for four years and had wanted to stop for a while. The doctor said: 'Why stop when it's working?', but it was around the time that we were thinking of starting a family: I didn't want to be dependent on medication for the rest of my life. I felt that it had helped me find a balance again.

I actually then came off the medication by accident. We went away on tour and I forgot to get a new prescription. We were in the middle of nowhere when I ran out and I had to go for a week without them. This is totally dangerous and I don't recommend it. Don't do this! I had a really dodgy couple of days but then suddenly felt okay. By the time I got home I'd gone for a couple of weeks without it and felt great, so I decided to see how it went staying off it. That was over two years ago now and I've never needed to go back. I've felt the best I have mentally felt in my whole life!

F: What do you do daily that keeps you in check and stops you from going down a slippery slope?

T: I eat pretty healthily now. That was a big change in my life. I'd struggled with weight a bit through the early years of the band and I think that added to the ups and downs. Once I got that in check and started looking after my body I found my mind felt much better, too.

The BIGGEST change though was sleep. I'd been terrified of aliens . . . yes, I know that sounds proper crazy... but it's true. It kept me awake EVERY night for the majority of my life and it was only when I got help for bipolar that I began getting help sleeping at the same time. Once I started getting proper sleep I found it much easier to deal with things that might trigger a low.

F: So your physical wellbeing seems to play a big part in your mental health?

T: Absolutely. If I'm feeling physically fit and healthy then my mind feels the same. I do a little ten-minute workout every morning on the bathroom floor before I shower and that is enough to get my heart racing and make me feel energised and ready for a good day. On the flipside, when I was feeling low I would purposely not look after my body. I'd eat rubbish, wear clothes I looked awful in, not shave, like I was physically turning into the way my brain was behaving.

F: Are there triggers that can bring on feelings of depression or bipolar highs?

T: Definitely. Whenever I'm writing or feeling really passionately creative I can feel myself getting caught up in a mild high period. This can last for a day, a week, a month. My 'ups' are very mild in comparison to what other people experience and, if I'm honest, I actually enjoy them – the hardest part is watching out for the lows.

These can be triggered by all sorts of things, although in my life they are usually set off by the disappointment of not achieving the impossible goal the 'high' me was trying to achieve. So, during the cycle of writing, recording and then releasing an album, I could quite easily trace my own cycle of ups and downs that followed the pattern of a yearly cycle of band life.

F: What does happiness mean to you? How do you access that inner joy these days?

T: It means everything to me because it's how I want my kids to see me. They are my joy and they are the reason I have to be the best version of me that I can be. I never want them to see me the way I've been in the past. They were totally the inspiration for me to sort my 'wonky brain' out and get my act together. I know it's not as simple as that for many people but by that I mean that I went and got help and spoke to people. Talking about feelings and emotions can be difficult, but I think my life changed the second I started being more open and honest about it.

F: Thanks for chatting with me today, lovely Tom. I really appreciate your honesty and time! You're one top bloke.

T: Aw, thanks! You ain't so bad yourself!

MENTAL VACATION

Giving yourself a mental vacation is a healing process whether we've had tough times or not. I often find that it's when I'm on holiday that I have those breakthrough moments. I either have good ideas for the future or epiphanies that lead to big change. These moments happen much less frequently at home when I'm constantly on the go with life and work. Extracting ourselves from our everyday routines and mental hamster wheel gives us space to think outside the box and perhaps be a little courageous.

So, how do we get to that place without the luxury of sitting by a pool with nothing to do? It's all about finding those short periods of time where you allow yourself space to breathe, time to heal, recharge and be still. These periods of time don't have to be lengthy or anything out of the ordinary. It's just about getting used to allowing yourself to BE and not DO. After all, we are human BEINGS not human DOINGS.

SEEK OUT PATIENCE

Having patience is another wonderful and overlooked tool that can help us in our quest for a happy balance. I'm sure we can all be honest: we are a generation of fast-living and demanding people who want an internet connection that's fast, shopping delivered quickly, trains to run on time and adverts fast forwarded, because we simply can't wait. We seem to have lost the ability, which means we're often aggravated.

I do it all the time. I'll be watching something in real time on TV and when the adverts hit I'll reach for my phone for a three-minute whirl of Instagram stimulation as my impatient mind spins at the idea of having to wait. But having the discipline to wait for things is a huge gift as the end result always feels better. It's that bit sweeter because we have to take the time to understand the work put in. We also absorb that much more from the experience due to the diligence needed to trust in the route taken.

I still feel I have many goals to accomplish and places I would like to go with my working life, but none of it has happened too quickly. It has taken me twenty years of work to get to where I am today, sitting here typing, and I'm thankful for every moment. I've lost jobs, been told I'm not good enough and lost all confidence and faith in myself at times. I'm sure at some point you've

We all place more importance on certain aspects of life, putting more energy into some over others. Here's your chance to address that **balance**.

Divide the first cherry up into the different areas of your life, be that work, school, family, exercise etc. Give each area the amount of space it currently takes up in your life, like a pie chart. Then divide the second cherry to your **desired balance**. What **changes** can you make to get your first cherry looking like the second?

experienced this in life, too. My approach now is to have faith and trust in the goal that feels good to me. Wait it out, practice patience and reap rewards in ways I hadn't expected.

A great example for me was my pregnancy with our second child, Honey Krissy. It was a treacherous nine-month wait, as I felt excruciatingly sick every single second of every day. I woke up every morning to a hybrid of seasickness and food poisoning that was debilitating and all-encompassing.

Reaching my due date and then going over it by three days felt like agony as I tossed and turned in the night, waves of queasiness drenching my every inch. But I managed to get out and about by thinking of each day as it came, rather than a never-ending road of gut-churning minutes and days stretching out before me.

Having Honey was the most beautiful experience, and I can now look back and feel a huge sense of wonder that mentally and physically we got through it together. It has made me appreciate having regular good health and simply feeling 'normal'. Understanding that I needed to develop the art of patience – and still do – was definitely a steep learning curve. But by looking at the bigger picture, the end game, patience can help us see our way through fears and pressures in life.

YOUR 'PEACEFUL' PERSON

Another very helpful hand comes in the form of your 'peaceful' person. Is there someone who instantly springs to mind who can calm your negativity in one fell swoop?

If you don't instantly recognise this person in your life, then maybe it's time to seek one out! They'll be there waiting for you.

Sometimes you might rather call the person you know will tip your imbalance further. I am guilty of this for sure. If I'm in a tetchy mood and feeling dramatic, I know certain people I can call or meet up with who will send me spiralling off further. But instead I try to turn to people who will bombard me with level-headed common sense and balance. One particular friend who I'm happy to mention is my mate Clare. She is a friend who approaches my own personal dramas with level, peaceful thoughts and truthful, balanced words. She sticks her head high above my own clouded vision and sees it all with a clarity I've lost along the way. I feel lucky to have her and others in my life who have become my go-to people when I need a little help. I appreciate these voices in my life very much, and hope at times I can offer them the same kind of support when they need it.

MY PEACEFUL PERSON IS: . . . .

Life can feel **messy** and unbalanced at times. Unravel your life imbalances and make peace with situations you cannot change by writing answers to the questions on the **string.**

WHAT FEELS OUT OF BALANCE IN YOUR LIFE?

HOW DOES THAT MAKE YOU FEEL?

WHAT FEELS IMPOSSIBLE TO CHANGE?

WHAT CAN YOU CHANGE?

SAY GOODBYE TO DRAMA

Avoiding drama is also essential on our pilgrimage to the land of balance. At times I adore a bit of drama; the sort I can dip my toe into – gossip about people I vaguely know or public figures. But this is very rocky ground to tread. Before you know it you've been sucked in completely and involved yourself in a story that you had little connection to in the first place but is now making you unnecessarily agitated or – if you know the people directly – that you now have to get yourself out of.

It's ironic, because we waste precious energy commenting on others' mishaps, forgetting that we've had many of our own. I've found surface-level judgement only attracts the same back, so now I try to remember my own tough times and mistakes and not judge other people's. I still fall into the trap of letting others' stories consume me when I really shouldn't, but mostly I'm very happy dealing with my own goings-on and those I love around me. If you want balance, say goodbye to drama you don't need.

Then, of course, there is the sort of drama that arrives in your life unbidden and unexpectedly, and when it happens all you can do is try to navigate your way out of it with the least possible damage to yourself and your heart. I have had drama lumped on me at times when I was looking the other way and wasn't ready. I don't react well e are likely to be the times when the big nd wraps its claws around my mind, whis- in my ear. If depression is on your personal rad ents like this will shortcut you to a place you hoped you wou revisit in a hurry. It was after my particularly dark patch had lightened and cleared that I knew I needed to say goodbye to self-inflicted drama forever.

Balance: an equation of patience, self confidence and discipline. We'll naturally sway off of it at times, but if we know the route back, we'll be okay.

Summary

TUNE INTO YOU.

Don't compare your wants or your time with other people's. Do what you want to do and make peace with FOMO.

YOUR INNER BAROMETER.

Listen to your gut. Understand your needs and breaking points and be aware of them.

TAKE TIME TO STOP.

Look around you. Try to be patient. Make space for the good stuff.

WHAT DOES HAPPY **BALANCE** LOOK LIKE TO YOU?

Write one word or draw a picture here that sums it up

HAPPY *Now*

What is it like to actually BE in the NOW? How does it feel to you? Without looking forward to something, regretting the past, covering tracks or thinking ahead, how do you actually feel? What can you hear, smell and see? How does your body feel? Being in the NOW brings you back inside your body, rather than continuously projecting forwards or backwards. The NOW is very powerful and allows you to invite all of those emotions and sensations in, rather than dulling them and ignoring them because your head is elsewhere.

RIGHT NOW . . .

I'm currently enjoying a full tummy from eating my dinner, my nose is taking in all of those foodie smells that make me feel at home and my body feels like it has done a lot over the past few days. It feels like it has had adventures and now needs a bit of rest. I'm happily writing away which sends my creative flow off in a nice rhythm that makes me feel calm.

As soon as I start to veer off and think ahead and beyond I can feel a slight anxiety fill my bones as I have a lot of work on tomorrow as well as caring for the kids and getting my house to look less like a jumble sale. This all feels chaotic and slightly overwhelming. I find bringing it back to the NOW is the key to calming those nerves and enjoying life in real time. Time feels as if it almost slows down as I savour every inhale and exhale.

Living in the moment doesn't necessarily feel that natural to us in this fast-paced day and age, does it? The future might seem tempting and limitless – where change is possible and dreams can manifest – or scary and chaotic as the unknown road ahead looks bleak and empty. Likewise, the past can bring us so much joy as we recall rose-tinted memories of blissful times where worries didn't exist and the sun shone constantly; but it can also be a place full of terror and regret that shouts so loudly you feel compelled to look back. But the

NOW is neutral. It holds no overwhelming emotion or concern, and I feel its importance and significance is often overlooked.

THE PROS AND CONS OF NOSTALGIA

For example, I don't know about you, but I'm terribly nostalgic. Good times I've had play out like a grainy movie with a delicious, harmonious soundtrack. A more relaxed me wafts through these scenes in a carefree manner, laughing and falling in love with everything around me. Sunsets were watched, drinks were drunk, adventure was ripe and the focus was soft.

I love reminiscing about certain points of my life that make me remember the carefree parts of my makeup that I can still easily access but sometimes get lost in the fog of family organising and work schedules. It's unlikely I'll pluck a memory of me booking train tickets or choosing a loaf of bread in the supermarket if I feel nostalgic, so my natural setting for reminiscing is to log into a seemingly 'better time'.

Dipping into a previous slice of your life is a joy, and is harmless as long as you remember that the version of you then is no better or worse than the one now. You have the capabilities and strength

We all have memories or situations that feel traumatic to recall. We bury them deep and try to forget, only for them to then jump out from the dark when we least expect. Here is the chance to **acknowledge, accept and make peace** with them.

What **memory** or thought brings discomfort to you?

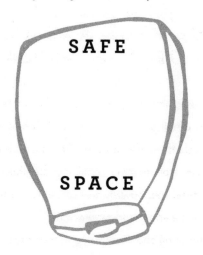

SAFE

SPACE

Which **one** word describes how this makes you feel?

· ·

And what one thing, even if very tiny, do you feel you've **learned** from that experience:

· ·

When this feeling or memory creeps up again try and **shortcut to the lesson**. That is the bit you can take away with your head held high. We can't make bad times disappear but we can twist our perspective to look at the tiny **silver lining** if we choose.

to be in control of your happiness NOW, just like you did back then. Don't compare your past to your NOW. Comparing always drains you. You'll tie yourself in knots as your sepia-tone memories outshine the possibilities of the NOW.

These feel-good scenes can also easily be pushed to one side by my own inner horror movie. This is the handful of memories that creep up when I'm feeling low or have a lack of confidence. They're there to tell me that I'm not good enough, that I've made bad decisions and that I don't deserve what I have. Like most people, I have a list of regrets and moments I would have played very differently today. Remembering them brings on a physical reaction that sees my skin redden, my shoulder muscles tighten and my throat contract.

Sometimes even the smallest regret can have this effect, as I worry and replay a mistake I've made at work until it becomes ten times bigger. This thought then dominates my confidence and self-belief as all positivity evaporates in a second. These mistakes swallow past work achievements and accolades in one sloppy bite.

Most of us have moments, no matter how big or tiny, that affect us greatly in life. It's inevitable that we will all make mistakes and experience things that we wish we hadn't. These good and bad memories will always live and breathe in our minds but it's how much we let them affect our everyday lives that is important. Do we let these thoughts and stories define us? Or can we see them for what they are: moments. Slices of time that occurred, had a directional purpose in our lives, then moved and changed into a new moment.

How do we stop bad memories from affecting our experience of TODAY? I think the answer lies in simplicity. One deep breath, one moment where you notice how things feel, smell and look around you, one positive thought to combat the negative story and one second where you remember that right now, in this moment, everything is just fine.

DON'T LET THE PAST
RULE YOUR DECISIONS

I think it's important to aim to make decisions and react to those around us from the NOW rather than the past. For example, maybe there's someone in your life who has constantly rubbed you up the wrong way and made you feel angry and agitated. When you see them and they say something that grates, you might be falling into your pattern of reacting in a negative way, as you're making that decision based on a past memory.

So long as we remember they are not more powerful than the now, recalling memories which **fill you with joy** is wonderful.

What five **memories** make you beam to recall?

1)
....

2)
....

3)
....

4)
....

5)
....

Maybe you worry too much in life. You are scared of flying or terrified you'll get ill. These fears often have their roots in the past. Maybe you had a frightening moment in the air, or saw those around you ill and scared somewhere along the way.

All of these past moments make up a pattern that you easily fall into as they become 'your ways'. 'I'm Fearne and I get overwhelmed when things seem chaotic. I get anxious when people judge me and am scared of picking up the phone when it rings as I expect it's bad news.' All of these characteristics feel bespoke to and part of me, whereas in fact they are all patterns I've picked up from past events. I grew up in a very ordered home where my mum kept the house neat and tidy which I guess felt safe and comforting to me, so now I have a need for order and to feel in control. I get anxious about people judging me because of years of being in the public eye and hearing many home truths as well as misinformed tales. I have had several devastating phone calls that have made me feel like the world was spinning in slow motion. This is why I hate to pick up my loudly ringing phone. My friends know to text or email me for a quick and happy response.

These aren't truths about who I am, they're patterns I've picked up from the past. If I can actually sit in the NOW and be in the moment by remembering that they aren't in control of me – I am in control of them – I know deep down it doesn't matter if the house is a bit of a mess, I know that people's opinions of me actually have no bearing on my life and self-worth, I know that the phone call could be from a happy friend who wants to say 'hi'.

The wonderful thing is, finding that awareness in a moment of panic, fear or worry could just be enough to start breaking these personal habits and patterns.

LOOKING AHEAD

Like many people out there, I get very caught up in 'the me of the future'. This version of me is carefree, more relaxed, laughing, mortgage-free, self-doubt free and living in a hot country.

It's fun and exciting to have these dreams and aspirations but I try not to let them define who I am today. Aiming high and having goals is exciting and buzzy as long as you know that the you of the future is no different from the person you are now. You may attain all you dreamed of, but there are no guarantees of happiness afterwards. You may achieve great success, own a home, complete a degree, get a job promotion – but still not feel any happier inside. We all get caught up in the fantasy of the future and how we will feel but this is the unknown – daily happiness has to come from the NOW. What we do doesn't make us who we are: it's very much how you do it, and the enjoyment you get from it daily. Reaching the end of the rainbow doesn't mean you'll be met by a better version of yourself, whereas getting happy NOW means you'll enjoy the whole journey a lot more!

If the future is a scary prospect to you then even more reason anchoring yourself in the present moment will be positive for you. If thinking ahead makes you feel as if a vast expanse of life lies in front of you without a plot, try sitting in the now. Let the fear dissipate and leave room for other emotions and energy. Again, it's about taking that brief moment to look around you, smell the coffee in the cup next to you, feel the clothes against your skin, look out of the window at the birds flying in the sky and be in the NOW.

WHEN YOU DON'T WANT TO BE IN THE 'NOW'

When we are going through tough times, being in the moment can be beyond uncomfortable, as all we want to do is escape our current mental location. This is when we reach for a numbing tool: food, alcohol, spending, gossiping, self-sabotage, judgement of others. They're all an attempt to get out of the now. If I feel edgy in the now, I want to eat snacks to numb my mind, I want to drink coffee to feel buzzy and I want to run to feel I'm moving out of the space I currently occupy. These are the things I turn to when I have this agitated sensation. Yet what I probably need in these moments is human connection. Sharing worries or a hug to release the tension. There's much more on this in the HAPPY SHARED chapter.

The singular thought I try to focus on in these times of discomfort is that this moment will expire. Like the cycle of day turning into night, or the circular motion of an inhale and exhale, this moment will come to a natural end. That's where change begins and something new is born. This thought somehow takes the pressure off and lets me relax in the knowledge that things change and bad times pass.

The tricky part of this is accepting the same with the good times. I have trouble letting go of those magical moments, as I want to hold on to them and keep them captive forever. But I like to think of those snippets of time as a perfume. Its delicious and intoxicating smell fades gradually until you can't detect its notes at all. It was beautiful and all-encompassing and then it faded. That's why these good times ARE so special – it's because they have an expiration date. They can't last forever and they remain dream-like because they come to an end. When we try to squeeze the life out of a good moment we hinder its ability to breathe and

Dreading future plans or situations can heap anxiety and fear right into your lap. If there's something that's worrying you, **share** it here.

. . . .
. . . .

What can you do or **change** to help diminish this fear?

. . . .
. . . .

Great – **do it**! If you can't make any changes, accept that, but know you **DO** have the strength and determination to get through what is ahead. Colour in the rising sunshine to add a bit of joy to your upcoming scenario.

drift in and out of our lives naturally. We must have faith that more of these divine love bubbles will float into our lives again. Be ready for the good and bad times with open arms, knowing they'll exist and then expire. In the meantime, all we can do is be in the NOW and take that big look around us.

DON'T RUSH AHEAD

At some point, we all rush ahead thinking: when that scary exam is over next week, 'I'll be okay' when that difficult impending conversation I need to have is done with, 'I'll be okay'. We speed through life wishing time and moments away, expecting to reach a happy, safe place. We are speeding up our own lives with this way of thinking. Do you remember the summer holidays when you were a kid? Six whole weeks off from school, which felt like six months? Endless days of sunshine and hanging with mates with the start of the next school year seeming so far off in the distance? That's because kids live in the moment, enjoying each fun pastime then moving onto the next one. Now time seems to whizz by because we are constantly looking ahead.

We can slow down our own experience and savour what life has to offer if we just sit in the now a little more often. In the present, our minds are clearer and not crammed tight with past and future anxieties. We can make decisions from a place of clarity and feel calm even when things seem chaotic around us. Stress is reduced and the feeling of being overwhelmed fades into the background. To me, that feels like a happy place to be.

Stop worrying about the past and fearing the future and get in to the **NOW**! Don't overthink these answers. Write down what **instinctively** comes to mind in this very moment:

Pick one thing you can **see** around you . . .

What can you **smell** . . .

How does your body **feel** . . .

What's **positive** about this very moment . . .

HELLO TO . . . KRIS

Every now and then in life, you stumble across someone who becomes very important in your story, and changes your outlook. Meeting Kris Hallenga was one of those golden moments for me. I had been on a Breast Cancer Care trek across Peru with a group of incredible cancer survivors, and one particular fellow trekking lady I got chatting to told me about the great support she had received from Kris and her charity, CoppaFeel! Kris was diagnosed with breast cancer in her twenties after initial misdiagnoses, and now makes it her life mission to get young women to know and check their breasts regularly. Her tireless work has helped thousands of women – and men – avoid going through what she herself had to endure.

After meeting Kris and witnessing her determination, tenacity and angel-like energy, I not only became a patron for CoppaFeel! but also gained a great friend. Kris and I have had many wonderful afternoons drinking coffee and chatting about life (cake makes an appearance quite a lot, too), we've danced wildly at my wedding, brainstormed ideas and future fantasies, and laughed a lot. Each time I hang out with Kris she inspires me in so many ways and breathes optimism and hope to all corners of the conversation. She faces problems, fears and nightmares head-on with courage, thought and grace.

We run events with Coppafeel! throughout the year but my favourite event is our annual music festival, Festifeel. Each year it grows and gains bigger headliners, more support from strangers and more smiles from the dancing revellers – and it all started as a single idea in Kris's head. It blows my mind each time I see these huge, love-filled CoppaFeel! events taking place. What a beauty she is and how lucky I am to have her as my friend.

KRIS: At twenty-two I was pretty miserable. Okay, maybe that's rather a strong word, but I certainly wouldn't have called myself 'happy' at the time. I was in a horrible relationship with a manipulative boy who made me feel worthless, I wanted a career in travel but just didn't know how to go about it, and my twin sister was a hotshot garden designer in a happy relationship. In short: I thought my life sucked. I guess I couldn't call myself happy back then, because I really didn't know what that word meant. I had been a happy child and a happy teenager, but when I hit twenty life became more of a pressure and, really, I couldn't stand to grow up.

At twenty-three I was diagnosed with incurable advanced breast cancer, and suddenly life and LIVING took on a whole new meaning. It shone a bright light on my mortality and what I still had to achieve while I was alive. I was no longer with my boyfriend and no longer felt I needed a man to make me happy– with cancer in tow, I had to start thinking about ME, how I could stay well, how I could fill my days with fun, good people and things that made me happy.

I started a charity called CoppaFeel! to ultimately ensure no one was dealt the same cards as me: being told they couldn't be cured because their cancer was found so late. I ploughed all my energy and time into the charity just two months after I was diagnosed and the buzz I felt when we got charity status is still the buzz I have today: it's the exhilaration that I believe has kept me alive this long (I'm now thirty, FYI). With cancer and running a charity I woke up every morning (okay, not EVERY morning) with a very good reason to get up. I lost a boob and the chance of a long life, but found a purpose. I have surrounded myself with wonderful people – because less than wonderful just won't do any more. I can steer my way to happiness much more clearly now than I could before cancer. I am more confident, which I would have liked to think has something to do with getting older, but I am content with my cyclops-boob body, my life, my mortality. But you know what? It shouldn't take cancer or in fact any shitty disease to make you realise how precious and wonderful life is; how being happy matters; how all the small meaningless shit doesn't.

But I would say I am the happiest I have ever been now, and although I don't recommend you all get cancer (it really is not fun, despite the hype) I truly hope you too can find happiness before, during and after whatever life throws at you. And check your boobs while you're at it.

Summary

THE PAST.

Enjoy your memories but don't let them rule you.

THE FUTURE.

Dream as you will but know happiness starts here, not there.

THE PRESENT.

Breathe it in and see what it has to offer. Enjoy its clarity, space and calm.

WHAT DOES HAPPY **NOW** LOOK LIKE TO YOU?

Write one word or draw a picture here that sums it up

HAPPY *Face*

Although happiness will always be found on the inside, our exterior has to be looked at, too. Our exterior is our projection. It's how we want to be perceived and can give a lot or little away. This chapter is not about make-up or vanity, but instead takes a step into the home of self-expression. It explores how we choose to display our true colours, or false ones, when needed. A lot of this, of course, lies in the mirror-laden underworld, more commonly known as social media . . .

HAPPY 'YOU'

How we look and dress can cause judgement on first sight. It can be a red herring that leads people to assume one thing about you while being distracted from another. Deciding how we want to look can be fun, but it can also be stressful and take up too much of our brain space.

When I was in my twenties I had a huge crisis of character. I felt I was too boring and too square to be desirable or fun, so felt the need to create a 'look' that made me seem more daring and adventurous than I truly felt. The first step was getting tattoos. It felt rebellious and exciting and, I thought, would surely make me look more that way inclined. I love most of my tattoos, as they remind me of particular chapters of my life and the people I've met, but some came from that place of wanting to feel more 'interesting'. Others later down the line came from a more considered place, and are much more a marker of a moment. I smile every time I look at those ones.

At this time of tattoos and rebellious behaviour I made friends with a group of cool kids and acted the part, although most of the time I secretly desired to be in bed with a book. I've had a lot of fun over the years but going out to clubs and bars has not necessarily felt that natural to me. I did it a lot in my twenties, but it never felt carefree and comfortable. It felt much more like something I should do to fit in, or be 'normal' (whatever that is).

I then dyed my hair every possible colour, imagining that I would then feel like a different person: someone who was fun and kooky and not so unnerved by the nighttime. It's only now that I write these words for the first time that I realise how much I don't like the nighttime. I love going to bed, and sleeping and relaxing, but going out at night never feels comfortable to me. The daytime feels fresh and new and full of opportunity, whereas the nighttime can feel tiring and a bit scary, although I can't put my finger on why. Pushing against this wariness of nighttime in my late teens and twenties makes me realise now how far from my own truth I was. I dressed, acted, and even started to think like someone else.

I view this decade, from our teens to our mid-twenties, as an experimental era. One where we are working out how we fit into the world, and how the world works around us. It's part of the adventure; finding out what makes you tick and what feels right to you. I just wish I had had the courage to be a bit more . . . well . . . ME! Most people find their way out of it sooner or later, but if you're stuck in a similar place now and have a desire to act in a more natural way to you, then go for it. If your actions are coming from a desire to please those around you or to simply fit in, work out how your life would change if you just did things your way. How scary is it to just be you?

FIND YOUR OWN
PEACOCK FEATHERS

I still love to experiment with hair colour, clothes and make-up, but now I'm not hoping it'll make me feel like someone else, I'm doing it all for fun: the fun of showing my peacock feathers and what I want others to see. On days when I feel confident, I'll dress in bright colours and clashing prints. On days where I have a nerve-wracking job, I may dress in an outfit that makes me feel strong and empowered. On days when I'm feeling blue or overwhelmed, I'll blend into the backdrop of life in black and baggy clothes that I can disappear into. I love that as humans we can be chameleons with the image we project, and how adapting that image can make us behave differently, too.

My heroes of popular culture, past and present, are all mavericks; individuals who don't (or didn't) give a hoot about what others think. David Bowie, Debbie Harry, Grace Jones, John Lennon, Jimi Hendrix, Vivienne Westwood, Beth Ditto, Tilda Swinton and Pam Hogg. They dress and present themselves in a unique way that causes reaction at every turn. Their style and confidence is admired and copied, and gossiped about and judged. They do this without fear and have no regard for the rest of the crowd. What a personally powerful place they must be in. My heroes walk through crowds, head held high and with an inner confidence, all honest and clearly enjoying every minute. Amen to that. I care much less what people think of me these days, but I would be lying if I said I was fearless. I like the visually quirkier side of life, but do feel I should tone things down sometimes so as not to be judged or berated. One friend of mine, who is the most adventurous and charismatic dresser, admitted recently that she – like me – sometimes tones it down at parties so as to prevent people staring and making judgements. To me, she seems fearless and full of fun, but she still has doubts and boundaries caused by what others might think. So, if that sounds like you, you're not alone!

FIND YOUR INNER FREAK

So get to know your own inner freak and invite them out to play. It takes balls to be unapologetically 'you' and project yourself from a truthful place: you need immense courage to speak your mind, go against the grain and present yourself in your own, bespoke way. But it also makes you feel very alive.

I fear that in this day and age we are all pushed and bullied into feeling like we have to act and look a certain way to 'fit in' or not be pulled apart by others. Welcome to the not so great part of social media.

Write down who your **hero** is. Someone who encourages you to release your inner maverick. Someone who goes against the grain for the good of themselves and others. Someone who **shines** no matter what.

THE GOOD, THE BAD, AND THE UGLY OF SOCIAL MEDIA

I am forever thankful that I started my career when I was fifteen, before the age of social media. I would go to work, have loads of fun, be happy if the show went well (or slightly disgruntled for a short while if it didn't), then I would get on with my day. In those days, if someone was watching TV or listening to the radio, they would – I'm sure – have had just as many opinions about what they were watching or listening to, but these thoughts would remain in their head, or maybe spoken aloud to a friend then forgotten. These days, if someone is watching TV or listening to music, those reactions are frequently expressed online for all to see. They remain, and they have staying – and even spreading – power. Once written and shared, words seem to intensify, strenghtening their meaning and intent.

Today, everyone is on show. We have Facebook, Instagram, Twitter, Snapchat, blogs and vlogs, and even if YOU don't engage with these social media platforms you'll probably end up on someone else's at some point. We are a culture of sharers. There's something lovely about this sharing – it's exciting and explorative – but its evil twin sister, judgement, looms large, too. We compare, scrutinise and see a small snapshot as something so much more.

I love whizzing through people's profiles, catching up with gossip on Twitter and generally procrastinating and escaping from my own reality. I enjoy looking at people's lives, getting inspired by clothing, drooling over food people have cooked and laughing at funny photos people have posted. I also love sharing parts of my own life online too. I enjoy having that control over how people view me and what I chose to portray. Instead of my life and stories being second-hand news from others' whispers, I can put my own opinions and ideas out there without the middle man's misinterpretation. There is something very powerful about having a community of people you haven't met all having a conversation about subjects you chose to put out there. It's interesting and engaging and I love that side of social media.

But sometimes I fall into the trap; I know the rules, I know the superficial truth of it, yet somehow I slip down that treacherous slope and get sucked into its fantasy world. And that's exactly what it is – a fantasy. When we watch a film at the cinema we can clearly distinguish between reality and fantasy. We know that the really hot lead actor is making us feel all gooey inside but equally we know we don't stand a chance with him and that's okay. We can fall hopelessly into a storyline, then leave the cinema and go back to our normal lives without taking that fantasy world with us.

With social media we all seem awfully confused, viewing what we see on the screen as hard fact. I've done it so many times: I'll be in bed early on a Friday night after a long and lovely day with my young children. I'll feel happy yet exhausted and so ready for a night of sleep in my old T-shirt and big pants. Just one look at Instagram won't hurt . . . will it? A constant supply of gorgeous people, dressed immaculately, looking so carefree and like they're having so much fun, while I'm in bed at 9.30pm and haven't even bothered to put proper pyjamas on. Therein lies the deathly vacuum of comparison and self-loathing. The little voice starts off quietly:

'I never bother going out any more, I am no fun at all. Look at my awful pyjamas that aren't even pyjamas. Everyone else is out there having a blast and they have the energy to do it. I am pathetic, here in bed at nine thirty on a Friday night.'

You scroll down further and see a famous face looking incredible in a bikini on a beach, eating a burger. The voice starts again . . .

'AS IF SHE IS EATING A BURGER! She has abs like corrugated iron. And . . . oh dear . . . look at my mum-gut. It looks like a deflated balloon the day after a party. I really should have gone to the gym tonight instead of reading *Vogue*. This weather is so awful too, why don't I live in a sunny climate where I can wear kaftans rather than duffle coats for ten months of the year . . . unbearable.' You are thrown between comparison and judgement, self-destructively swinging from one to the other.

Why don't we all look at these moments of other people's lives and see them as fantasy, like we do when we watch a film at the cinema? Plus, those gorgeous people at the party may just have had the most awful day. They may be clutching that rather large cocktail for dear life as they wash away their inner turmoil; they may really not like the person they are cuddling in the shot, and wish they had not worn those really tight trousers as their period has just started and they feel really bloated. Hot famous face on the beach with her burger may feel incredibly insecure, as she is judged solely by her looks. She tucks into her burger, wishing others would look beneath the skin to see who she really is. She might be on holiday, soul-searching as she had some bad news before she left, and actually the sun is rather too hot and has given her an excruciating headache. Who knows . . . it was a moment. It passed and it should hold no other significance other than: it happened.

You may have seen photos on my own social media channels that have made you think I have it all sorted. Well, let me reiterate that I most certainly do not. As I write this book I'm still learning to live in this way. I'm learning to take a step back, to look at what's really going on and to react accordingly. There may be a photo or two of me on social media that I've posted where I'm in a lovely frock and happen to be smiling in a flattering way. I guarantee you that an hour before those shots were taken I was struggling to get my three-year-old to eat dinner while my daughter smeared her pasta-sauce-covered hands up the wall, while I simultaneously tried to take a quick urgent work call and also desperately needed a wee. That was the reality of my day, not the shot of me in a nice dress. It's all completely misleading if taken seriously. With social media we can portray ourselves and our lives however we wish, underplaying or exaggerating what we wish, for all to believe.

DANCE TO YOUR OWN BEAT

Alongside this self-comparison and judgement comes the fear of dancing to our own beat. We get scared to be different. It's like being back at school where you're very aware of everyone around you and how they're acting. Selfies should be taken at a certain angle, anything remotely imperfect should be hidden, and clothing should be a certain way so that the LIKE icon is pressed as many times as possible.

This element of social media drives me mad. Firstly, I worry that younger generations, who have been born in the era of social media, will base their own self-worth on how many LIKEs they receive. This new currency is dangerous: we should all want to do things because they feel meaningful and in tune with our hearts rather than because everyone else likes it.

Secondly, I worry that anything 'different' or 'unique' is viewed as negative. But why on earth would we all want to be the same as each other? We should celebrate our unique features and show the world how great they are.

I sometimes wonder if we've forgotten that beauty is subjective. When did the lines blur so much that beauty now seems to be one particular thing, a list of requirements that has to be met? If we all shared the same opinion of what beauty is, then we would all be desperately fighting for the same life partners, friends, and stuff. Beauty is of course a word we define personally: our own instincts push us towards people and things that have a magic around them that can't be explained. I worry that the way we are using social media will eventually make this theory extinct. It holds up one type of acceptable beauty, whether that be a person's face, a collection of objects, an outfit or an idea. Anyone who dares to show their own version of beauty is criticised, and told they don't fit in. Everyone is entitled to an opinion but, on social media, comments are often written as definitive facts: 'that's not beautiful', 'that's ugly', 'that's horrible'. But beauty is subjective; someone out there will think the subject at hand IS beautiful.

I have relatively unattractive feet, which doesn't hinder me or bother me in any way, but if I ever post a photo of them, to show off a luscious pair of shoes, I get several comments about the state of my feet. Now, I'm very proud of my feet. They've kept me walking for thirty-four years so far and allow me to run, dance, do yoga, oh . . . and wear those dreamy shoes. But apparently, because my feet don't resemble those in a nail varnish advert, they're labeled as 'bad'.

Luckily, I'm old enough and have been through enough real trauma in life not to worry about people's judgement of my slightly squished and bulbous little toe, but I'd be lying if I said other general comments don't bother me. If people view my social media and write a comment that I feel doesn't correlate with either the story I was trying to tell or the actual truth, I feel hurt and out of control. If someone says I'm bad at my job, I feel dented and my ego speaks up in an angry, pained voice. I am affected by it but after a while, once I've had a chance to process it, I find myself able to locate where that hurt is coming from. I now know that it's not about the person that threw their own fears my way, it's coming from a deeper, tucked away corner of my mind where I share those same thoughts and feelings about myself. We are all our own worst critics, and I can recognise this and work through

Judgement and unkind words towards us is tricky terrain to navigate. Working out where those words came from, and why they were spoken, helps to **dilute** these negative feelings and move on from it all.

How did you **feel** the last time someone said something negative about you?

What do you think made them say it? (**Hint** . . . it'll be more about them than it is about you 😊)

that acute fear and move on a lot quicker than I used to.

I know some people are affected more severely by these sorts of comments online, however, so I believe understanding these weird stereotypes and rules set by social media is crucial. If we know that modern-day stereotypes are just that, and that we don't have to conform to them – well I think that is liberating and freeing. Remember to go with those moments when you FEEL beautiful, when you FEEL happy and glowing from the inside: these moments are the ones worth celebrating and sharing.

Be brave, be bold, be you, and dance to your own beat.

DIGITAL DETOX

I don't know about you, but I think most of us spend too much time on our phones, or looking at screens. We use them to communicate, procrastinate, shop, search, view. It can be a lot of fun, but can also have a negative effect on our lives, not just because of all the comparisons we make with all our Insta-friends, but also because it makes it tricky to concentrate on being in the NOW. It's non-stop, so knowing when to put those screens away is vital. Having kids makes this much easier, as when I'm looking after them both it's near impossible to have a free hand or eye to look

Choose a time that feels right to step away from your phone. Physically place your phone over the outline on this page and don't touch it for a **whole hour.** See how you feel, what thoughts arose and how much you saw around you without your phone. A good old **daily digital detox** does us all the world of good. We switch off from a world of media and see what's going on around us with clarity. Give it a try!

at my phone. But, at other times, I often need to be reminded to put my phone down. Before bed I try to not look at social media, as I know it'll spark my thoughts off in several directions when it should be headed down a calm, one-way street to sleep land.

I also think phones and mealtimes shouldn't go together. When you're having dinner with your family or friends, the phone needs to take a back seat, so that you can communicate with your companions and read their faces as well as hear their words. I also think it's good to go cold turkey for certain periods of time, just to see if it changes your mindset. One year, when my husband Jesse and I were on holiday, we had our phones stolen. This happened on the first night, so for over a week we had no access to social media, no cameras and limited communication tools. It felt horrible and disconcerting at first, but after about three days I felt so much calmer and much more in the moment. We have no photos of this trip, but instead I have vivid, sun-kissed memories and I love that having no photos to share makes the holiday almost feel secret. Those memories are for us to reminisce about and not for the consumption of anyone else. I love sharing photos, but that unexpected (and unwanted) experiment had many surprising upsides. Perhaps you know you're on your phone too much and are intrigued about what it would feel like to experience spans of time without a flurry of communication and thumb ache. If so, give the digital detox on the previous page a go.

What's perfect got to do with it?

I'm flawed. I make mistakes. I have hurt people. I sometimes judge others. I say stupid things. I go red easily. I have been naive. I have regrets (and a couple of regrettable tattoos). I often don't like how I look in photos. I've been drunk for the wrong reasons. I can be impatient. I lose perspective at times.

Who doesn't?

This is me.

Now write your own list here ...

Then celebrate them!

YOUR TRUE COLOURS

Have you noticed how young children have no filters or concerns as to what's going on around them? They splash in puddles, shout when they want something, dress in loud colours, speak honestly and openly, and don't think ahead. There's much we can learn from this. I watch my own children and stepchildren and admire how their minds work as they move from one fun moment to the next, constantly seeking joy and fun without inhibitions.

Showing our true colours, in whatever way we can, is vital to being authentic and deep-down happy. Doing things your own way and braving it is thrilling and exciting. Friends of mine that have this courageous streak are my most inspiring heroes in life: friends who have been honest about and proud of their sexuality; friends who have fought illness with courage and sent out strong, loud messages for others to take note of; and friends who have gone against the grain and followed their heart, whether that's taken them abroad or to areas of work that seem less stable or comfortable.

Personally, I've always been drawn to doing things a bit differently, as it encompasses a sense of freedom and liberation I can't find elsewhere. I like to surprise people, and even myself, by going with my gut and doing things my way. When I was just seventeen I saved and saved until I could afford a flight to go and meet my cousins in America that we, as a family, had lost touch with. I'd only ever corresponded by letter with my cousin who is the same age as me, and had no idea how the whole experience would play out (having never met them before). Neither I nor my parents had left Europe, so the whole idea seemed slightly bonkers at the time. I only panicked once, when the plane was landing in Los Angeles, but I'm so glad I followed my gut and sense of adventure, as I'm now great friends with that side of the family and have been out to visit my cousin several times since. That trip remains treasured in my memory bank: the teenage me sitting in an old-school American diner sipping cherry cola while eating fried zucchini, just one of many new and strange experiences that felt thrilling and expansive. I can reminisce fondly and remember how exciting life can be when you embrace your true colours.

But when I look back, I know there are lots of times when I haven't: I've taken on certain jobs because I felt everyone else would think it looked good. I've bitched about people to feel accepted in certain circles. I've gone along with others' opinions so as not to rock the boat. I've been sucked into obsessing about what I should be achieving and doing, and then felt the inevitable self-loathing as I realise I don't match up to others. I've spoken words that weren't from the heart; said things that I thought were right but that were not real or true. These are all moments I look back at with a crippling cringe. They bring out a physical reaction in me, as I know I wasn't being true to myself. Even writing this book has brought on huge sweats of panic, as I lose my way and fall into a well of self-doubt and fear. My mind has whirred with worries that others will mock me for my efforts or rubbish my stories and ways of thinking. When I get back on track I remember that fundamentally this is all coming from the heart so, whether it's viewed positively or negatively, it has felt very right to me. That's all you can do in life. Follow what you believe to be true and it will always lead you back to that place of happiness and light.

I will never be one of those people who has no regrets, but I will hopefully, one day, get to a place where I can make peace with all of them. I will be able to see them as precarious stepping stones that have led me to where I need to be. They've fast-tracked a lesson I needed to learn and made me stop and digest what's going on around me. I'm not quite there yet, as some of these inauthentic

moments still cause me to flush when I recall them. Maybe this place of acceptance comes in time, with age, experience, and life laundry. We grow, learn and accept so that we can move through life with ease and precision and can make the most of this precious time we have here on planet Earth. I look forward to when I can look back and accept it all: the good, the bad and the inauthentic.

SPEAK UP AND LIVE
FEARLESSLY

Lastly, the tricky bit. If we don't want people to make snap judgements about us, then we shouldn't make snap judgements about them. When people are acting differently to how you deem appropriate it is hard not to cast them as the villain in your story. Unfortunately, there will always be people out there who are not acting from the heart and will cause others pain and suffering by their actions; someone you don't know or people that feature in your own personal narrative. Maybe you don't agree with a family member's way of thinking, or a friend's behaviour or means of expression. Rather than view what they are doing as wrong, I think it's better to try and see it from their viewpoint. Why have their decisions felt right to them? Are they acting from an authentic place, driven by love? If not, then why not? What are they scared of? Asking these questions has helped me to understand others better and not vilify them.

We all get a slight kick from pointing out other people's mistakes in life, probably because it makes our own less prominent. Unfortunately, it doesn't work like that at all. It doesn't make our own mistakes vanish, nor does it make us any better as individuals. If you can recognise mistakes or cracks in other people's lives, surely it's far better to think back to your own, and acknowledge why you made those choices at that time. You might then find peace with your own miscalculations in life.

I endeavour to act from the heart. If you feel doing the same will bring joy and happiness into your life, why not give it a go,

THE MOST
AUTHENTIC
YOU

Doing what truly floats your boat will always allow you to be the most authentic version of YOU and in turn feel a lot happier in life. Write down a wish or hope on the stepping stones, no matter how big or tiny, and know that they'll get you that bit closer to the authentic you who is led by the heart.

too. Why not speak up and say your heart-felt bit when people in your friendship circle talk negatively of others? Why not do things that make you happy, even if they're not the norm? Why not wear what you really want to, so that you can show how you're feeling inside? Why not live life fearlessly? I'm certainly going to keep on trying.

Summary

SHOW YOUR PEACOCK FEATHERS.

Work out what feels right to you, and don't be afraid to show it.

UNDERSTAND SOCIAL MEDIA.

Recognise it's not a reflection of real life; it's just a snapshot.

STRIVE FOR THE AUTHENTIC YOU.

Learn from the past, steer away from negativity and be fearless.

WHAT DOES HAPPY **FACE**
LOOK LIKE TO YOU?

Write one word or draw a picture here that sums it up

HAPPY *Choices*

Being free to make choices is what makes life exciting. We are able to change our lives, head off in a new direction and change our state of mind if we wish. A millisecond. That's all it takes. A fraction of time where you stop and make a choice, commit to it and feel at peace with it. If we even start to be aware of the power of this small dot of time, it can be a huge game-changer.

THE POWER OF CHOICE

Having choice is the ultimate freedom, but sometimes we forget we have it, especially when life is tough and change and choice seem to go out of the window. When you don't like something in life, are you the sort of person who feels like change is impossible and uncomfortable? Or do you go about making changes to see where that takes you? It's not always easy, and sometimes we are trapped in situations which can take a long slog to untangle ourselves from. But when I've managed to take control of a bad situation and initiate change, even if it's a tiny one, I've felt safer, more balanced and happier; you don't have to think too big on this one. Just remember you have the freedom to make changes and have every right to enjoy the power of those moments freely.

One amazing example of the power of choice is recognizing that we can choose HOW to react to situations. We react to what is going on around us all the time. We react if someone is mean about us, we react if something tempting swims in our direction, we react when our ego is dented. It's something we've grown up seeing our parents do, it's part of being a small child, it's in films we watch and songs we listen to. But the great thing is, the way we react to any given situation may feel subconscious or like a reflex, but in fact we can choose how to react: in a positive way, a negative way, or not at all.

Although I'm a relatively calm person at this point in my life, I still struggle with anger. I can feel a rush of bright red to my face, followed by a tingling in my chest and a tension in my hands. The rage is palpable and in those moments feels like it has taken over. I've lost control, my brain is on fire and all normality ceases to exist around me.

There are several reasons I will get swallowed up by this red-hot lava, but luckily I'm now at a point where I can quickly locate the truth of the situation.

I like to be in control. I feel safe and comfortable when things around me look how I expect them to look, and I find it easier to navigate through terrain I understand and view clearly. As soon as there's a tremor in this fragile landscape I easily lose my footing and my head spins, sending a tension through my body as I try to grasp control of the situation. This affects me both on a large and tiny scale. If my house is a mess I feel disorientated and OUT of control. I will feel a small rage flaming up when I know I haven't the time to sort it out immediately as my regular safety settings seem off and treacherous.

If someone says something untrue about me, I spiral into an inner anger, ranting and puffing knowing there's nothing I can do.

Obviously, in the job that I do, this is a regular occurrence, but is one I still don't deal with very well. And if I see or hear of people being treated unfairly, I rant for hours about the injustice and ignorance, and let this rage physically wind me up until I'm exhausted.

TAKE BACK CONTROL

In these moments I've forgotten that I have a choice. I can backtrack and work out where this rage is truly located and I can step outside the fire pit, and react differently. This doesn't mean I can extinguish the fury immediately, but I'm getting there.

I see now that getting angry is my choice, so when I can, I choose not to let it rule me. That, ironically, is the ultimate control. I get angry when I feel OUT of control, whereas I could choose not to feel the anger and be instantly IN control.

If you have an emotion or trait that makes you feel out of control, then you can give this a go, too. Your go-to reaction could be jealousy, fear, low self-esteem, aggression. Even though these overriding feelings may seem like they're running the show, if you make changes, you can learn to live with your natural Achilles heel without letting them take over.

RECOGNISE THE ROOTS

So how do you choose not to react? I think the first step is working out WHY you jump to that reaction. So with me, for example, if my house is a mess, what I'm worried about is that everything looks as messy as it sometimes feels in my head. This visible mess seems to heighten the jumbled thoughts in my brain which reach fever pitch. So now I try to use that millisecond to stop and CHOOSE – rather than feel rage, I'll take a moment to notice that actually, I feel internally a bit all over the shop. The kitchen sink can wait and I can try to sit with those uncomfortable feelings of inner turmoil. That's the tough bit we all struggle with . . . sitting with it. More on this in a moment.

When someone says something untrue or mean about me I can again choose to use that millisecond of time to delve back to where this is really hurting. I'm taking it personally rather than seeing that the person who is judging me is perhaps just lashing out due to their own issues. I doubt they're really that invested in my life story; they're merely projecting their own worries onto me, as it's much easier than sorting their own situation out.

Rather than use precious energy on firing up the anger engine I can use that millisecond to let go and know that it truly doesn't matter how others view me. I still find this one very tricky but I'm aware of it all, which is a great starting block for progress. In that moment I can try to send that person love instead of anger as they're obviously hurting, too.

SIT WITH YOUR EMOTIONS

If I've made the decision to not react with anger when someone is unkind to me and opted instead for a compassionate and empathetic mindset, I now have to examine WHY their comments affected me so much. Does my ego feel dented? Do I believe some of what was said to be true? We all deal with 'sitting' with mountains of emotional upheaval in different ways. Do you reach for a glass of wine to numb the pain? Raid the biscuit tin to fill an emotional hole? Hit the gym to run away from it? Go shopping to distract yourself and bring something new to the situation? There are so many physical reactions that we habitually gravitate towards when we are faced with the undercurrent of emotions running the show.

I'm not, of course, saying don't ever eat a biscuit again! There is a big difference in choosing to do these things from a place of discomfort rather than from a place of joy. But if you are hitting up these habits from a place of discomfort, ask yourself how bad would it be if you just sat with those feelings and made peace with them, or at least tried to, instead? How would we feel if we didn't numb what we know is there in front of us with our 'go-to' habits?

Maybe it wouldn't be as bad as we all subconsciously imagine. Maybe when we have sat with that discomfort and let it come and go naturally, we can then start to really understand how we feel about certain fears and worries – and then we can begin to make decisions that will dilute them in the future. These milliseconds almost defy how we see the clock ticking, as such huge changes can occur in these tiny nuggets of time. Remembering we are in control of our reactions and that we are responsible for how we deal with the outcome can be a huge help to us all. We are awoken to the fact that we can mould our own story if we choose.

SWITCHING IT UP

Is there something in life that doesn't feel quite right at the moment? Is it a job, a partner, a location, a friendship? It might feel immovable and stuck, but there is always a choice. A change that can take place, to take you off in another direction. This could be a big life change or just a change of mindset. If there is a situation in your life you cannot change, the switch-up will come from you

Write within this outline anything that is making you feel uncomfortable in life. Rather than numbing or burying that feeling or situation, **sit with it**. Get to know it better, understand it better, and make peace with it.

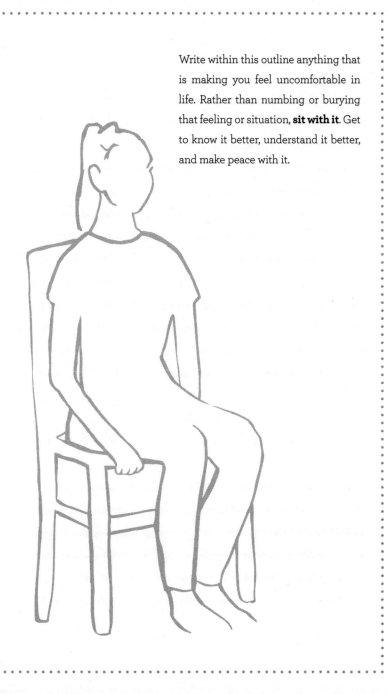

YOU CAN DO It (even if you think you can't)

accepting this, rather than butting your head against a wall constantly hoping for something new.

If you know there is room for change, then what is stopping you? Fear of the unknown? Other people's opinions? Lack of confidence? If you know making a change will lead you to unlocking your inner happiness then GO FOR IT.

When I left Radio 1, I had so many people tell me I was bonkers. I knew it was a brilliant and prestigious job, and I knew it was a safety net for me, but I also knew deep down that I craved change. It wasn't coming from a negative place where I needed to get out; I simply wanted something new, and believed I had the choice to go where these desires were pushing me. When I made the jump after ten years there I was petrified and it felt very odd, but now I'm doing so many new and different things that have expanded my mind and led me to meet new people.

I've also had people in my life who have seemed problematic. Individuals who haven't brought out the best in me, and who presented me with many reasons to act from a non-authentic place. Some I have been able to move away from naturally and without too much trauma. Others, who I can't remove from my story, I deal with from a distance and from a detached mindset. I try not to get emotionally hooked in, as I know it's dangerous territory. In both circumstances, I have acknowledged the place those individuals have in my life and have then CHOSEN to do something about it.

If you're feeling the potential for a big life change on the horizon but still can't quite take your first step off the diving board then, for now, take small considered steps. You don't have to make great leaps from the get-go. Work out what you feel needs to change and make your choices around that. Decide which tiny stepping stones can set you in the right direction, but won't feel like a shock to the system. If you know your inner happiness will improve with change, grab those choices by the horns and breathe in the unknown.

ASSESS YOUR CHOICES

When I was in my twenties, I had one goal, and that was to be as successful career-wise as I could be. I don't think I took a second to work out why I wanted this. Much later down the line, I can put the pieces together and work out what was really going on.

It wasn't about affluence and fame, as I grew up in a working-class family where that sort of lifestyle wasn't on my radar. I had a happy childhood with everything I needed: family love, food, the odd camping holiday and a few after-school hobbies.

Instead, I think it was that the younger, wrinkle-free me wanted to feel like I was living every moment to the max. At first I dreamed of making it in the entertainment industry as I had a need for excitement and this line of work seemed to tick all the boxes. Once I had a foot in the door, my perspective changed. I was having new and exciting experiences but still felt they lacked something. Now it was all about feeling, deep down, how I imagined everyone else in the industry felt. Powerful, confident and like they belonged. I felt so out of place, and often like I had fallen into the television screen, surrounded by people I watched who were all aware of how alien it all felt to me.

I now know what I'm searching for and why, but back then I was scrambling to find that place where I felt comfortable and in control. I thought by reaching for the biggest shows, scariest jobs or an amount of work that allowed no rest, I would feel complete. It was loads of fun and brilliantly bonkers but I became jaded at times, as I dulled my own inner light and excitement by not always following my gut.

Now, I am a happy mum and have experienced a vast array of weird and wonderful broadcasting work, and I know what my goal is. My dreams now lie in the hands of creative flow and feel-good actions. I want to be part of a movement of people that feels good and joyful. This can come in many forms, from just simply

Are you finding it hard to make a **decision** in life? It could be a huge life decision that is causing you sleepless nights or something **trivial** that is bugging you. No matter of its size write it down here:

. . . .

... and fill out the Pros and Cons to see which list gains more traction!

PROS

CONS

. . . .

. . . .

. . . .

. . . .

. . . .

being with my family, TV shows that have a great cast and crew bond, a radio job where I can hope to transport some good energy through the airwaves, or a creative project like this book where I can connect with lots of other people. Being part of something and using my mind in this way feels good. So I'm sticking with it.

CHOOSE POSITIVITY

Seeing others get hurt or be mistreated is tough to deal with, particularly as this strange ball we are floating on seems to have endless conflict and pain doused all over it. We are reminded daily of the horrors faced by some on this planet due to war or lack of basic neccessities.

What we need to remember is that there are equal measures of magical and wonderful things happening, but we tend to hear more about the negative. When I hear these stories, instead of ranting and getting myself physically worked up, I can stop, and send a prayer, a good thought, or a wish for those who truly need it. Anger is a waste of time and serves no one. Putting weighty mind-power to good use is a much healthier option and a great choice in those moments when we feel drawn in by the seduction of ranting or gossip.

Grab a pencil and spin it over the **wheel of joy.** Then go about making this positive happen in your life! Putting a **positive spin** on what's going on in our lives is a quick way to inject a bit of happiness.

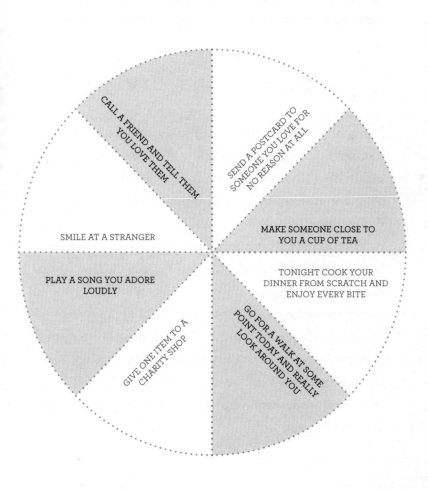

CALL A FRIEND AND TELL THEM YOU LOVE THEM

SEND A POSTCARD TO SOMEONE YOU LOVE FOR NO REASON AT ALL

SMILE AT A STRANGER

MAKE SOMEONE CLOSE TO YOU A CUP OF TEA

PLAY A SONG YOU ADORE LOUDLY

TONIGHT COOK YOUR DINNER FROM SCRATCH AND ENJOY EVERY BITE

GIVE ONE ITEM TO A CHARITY SHOP

GO FOR A WALK AT SOME POINT TODAY AND REALLY LOOK AROUND YOU

Writing down a **list of positives** will always lead you to happiness. It gives you time to recognise the good things in life, which in turn **attracts** more of those things as you concentrate and focus on what makes **you feel great.** It's win-win!

Your positive list ... GO!

1)

2)

3)

4)

5)

6)

7)

8)

9)

10)

Being notified of others' pain of course makes all of us stop and ask WHY? It seems so very unfair and unjust. But if we are fuelled by a particular story, we can make a positive choice to DO something, using that frustration and energy to do good. I feel very lucky that my line of work has allowed me many experiences where I have been able to use that sorrow for injustice to do some good. I have met some of the most incredible people through my job who have been hit by poverty, illness or loss, and I have gained monumentally from them, too. I've learned so much, stripped back my own fears and been witness to hugely inspiring mega-watt strength. These transactions of goodwill could be a small gesture, such as sending a letter to someone in hospital that'll make them smile and feel loved in that moment. It could be a charity run or fundraiser. You could even just call someone who you know is lonely. Far better to get up and do something about all the injustice on this planet, rather than just ranting about it.

Helping, of course, feels so good, too. That's the other magical part of reaching out. You are making a change to someone else's life but you're also making changes to yours. The satisfaction you feel from these acts is unbeatable.

There are so many kind and thoughtful people out there who make huge changes to others' lives and these wondrous humans are some of the happiest I know and they will forever inspire me.

And – don't forget – change is incredibly powerful when we all get together. More people thinking in a certain way and wanting change can move mountains.

FIND YOUR POSITIVE OUTLOOK

Being positive isn't always easy. It's sometimes the harder route, the one that requires more energy, thought and commitment. Personal patterns of self-deprecation, sorrow and anger are easier to slip into. When these negative thoughts are swimming around, we can't join the dots and see why things aren't going well, because we are so focused on what is lacking and depleted.

In today's culture, you almost have to go against the grain to think positively. We are constantly reminded of what we are 'lacking', through advertising and the need to compare ourselves to others. This leads us down a negative path of seeing only what's missing. We forget to look for the positives, we don't fully open our eyes to the good that is in front of us. I believe that focusing on the positives, and learning to accept the parts of life you can't change, is the road that will lead you to a happier life. Getting your mind working in a positive way allows you to be a lot calmer and make decisions from a solid place.

I do sometimes struggle with this and can find myself in a state of panic when things feel like they're not going how I imagined they would. I beat myself up and forget that it's okay to make mistakes or to go off on a tangent in life. When I'm feeling like this, speaking to those who have seemingly cracked this mindset helps massively. My husband is one of those people. He can calm my chaotic anxiety in minutes with his broadened outlook on life and love. I need anchoring like this, so feel forever grateful I have that person so close to me. He pulls my spinning kite out of the storm and roots me again. That's the feeling I like. Grounded, sturdy and balanced.

I feel lucky to have a lot of people in my life who choose to have a positive outlook and an open mind, from whom I can constantly learn.

HELLO TO . . . CRAIG

One of the most positive people I know is my friend, Craig David. I have
known him through various stages of his career, personal life and fame, but
one thing that has remained constant and solid is his outlook. He hasn't
compromised his vision or ethics to shortcut his route to happiness and
doesn't care what anyone else thinks or says. That takes guts and self-ac-
ceptance in great doses. I had a chat with Craig to hear what really makes
him tick and what keeps him on this path.

**F: I've known you for many years now, Craig, and you've always been
one of the most positive people I know. What keeps your head in this
space and can it be difficult at times?**

C: I feel the same about you, Fearne. Over the years I've been able to see
that the things that really make me happy are so simple, yet sometimes we
tend to overlook them. I'm just grateful to wake up in the morning and be
healthy, surrounded by my friends and family, have a roof over my head,
food on my table and clothes on my back. Add the fact that I'm so blessed
to be able to express myself through music every day and touch so many
people's lives – it's hard to not be buzzing off life.

**F: You've got great self-belief and that has allowed you to be patient
in your approach to your own creativity. How do you hold your nerve
when everyone else around you thinks differently?**

C: I've found it's really about being comfortable with leaning into the unknown where most would find it uncomfortable. Yes, it can be a little scary, but it's where all the magic happens. As for holding my nerve, I've come to learn that no one really knows what you're striving for deep down except you, so by following your intuition and surrounding yourself with positive people that support you and your vision you create the right environment for ideas to manifest.

F: How do you personally block out the noise of negativity around you or do you digest it and use it in a beneficial way to your own life?

C: Putting my headphones on and turning the music up LOUD seems to work . . . it blocks everything out. LOL! What I've come to understand is that we will always experience negative people and situations, but the key is to be able to see what can be learnt from them and to be aware and brave enough to remove what is causing the negativity from your life. I know it's easier said than done, but what I found extremely helpful was to be able to look at the negative situation and then see what I could change in myself that would make the external circumstances better.

What is the key to your own personal happiness?

F: Sharing what I have. Loving those around me. Receiving love back. Being creative and letting light shine through me. Learning and unfolding as I go has to be the biggest adventure that awakens that happiness.

Has something little irritated you today? If **yes**, what was it?

. . . .

Now choose to see that situation in a different light. Make the choice to find a **positive**, whether that's a learning about yourself or a consequence of the situation.

. . . .

. . . .

. . . .

. . . .

Summary

TAKE THE MILLISECOND.

Give yourself a chance to make the choice about how to react to a situation.

TINY STEPS.

If you're itching to make a change, make tiny steps in its direction!

FIND POSITIVITY.

Make the choice to see the positive rather than the negative in situations.

WHAT DOES HAPPY **CHOICES**
LOOK LIKE TO YOU?

Write one word or draw a picture here that sums it up

HAPPY *Mind*

A happy mind, to me, is a breeding ground for opportunity and positivity.
It is a place where positive options outweigh the negative. It is a muscle
that has the ability to mould your life into one of contentment and joy.
The mind can be so wonderful with its ability to dream, invent, create and
imagine. A hub, continuously growing and facilitating change, revolution
and action. When we use our minds in a positive way we can dream, act
and create with ease.

CREATING A HAPPY MIND

A lot of the time we forget the mind is something we have an element of control over. It's easy to feel it's running the show, and it sometimes escapes from its leash and gallivants off into unwanted territory. We either feel unable to tame the mind's unruly nature or we believe certain patterns and ways in which it works are set in stone, because 'that's just how we are'.

As I touched on earlier, what we forget is that we made up the rules. We learn as kids the difference between right and wrong and what we deem suitable but the rest is up to us. We can create our own story, and it doesn't have to go in just one direction.

We have learned that we have certain traits and hold on to those labels tightly. For example, we may be sensitive to criticism, or perhaps we feel overwhelmed when faced with certain tasks. These are all traits we have told ourselves we own: they're ours. Our ways of thinking are somehow etched into our very core. We tend to forget that we can shake up our own internal system to something different whenever we please.

As we all know, it's impossible to be fully in control of life, as we wake to the uncertain every day. The world is spinning with us sitting on its surface, waiting to see what it will throw our way. It could be adventure, opportunity, a fateful meeting, a loss . . .

we just don't know. We have to be able to adapt to what is taking shape around us. We can start to feel control over our own destinies when our minds are not working single-handedly, but as part of our whole body and soul.

Making decisions, feeling emotions, speaking the truth, loving wholly, acting authentically, all come from using the WHOLE of you. Your mind, body, and that extra bit of magic you can't quite put your finger on. We have to align all these parts of us in order to make the decisions we know deep down will benefit us.

TRAIN YOUR BRAIN

Using your mind in this way requires a bit of dedication and discipline as you learn to train it to work in a positive way. When I'm feeling negative I know that by habit I tend to seek out more negative. I forget that I can switch this up whenever I choose. I can smile rather than scowl, and I can look for the beauty in what is going on around me, rather than seeing just the darkness.

This will in turn attract more happiness and positivity, as you're seeing it everywhere. Light attracts light.

BACK IN THE DRIVING SEAT

Getting your mind into good healthy habits, like we do physically with our bodies, is integral. We go to the gym to get toned, but rarely think about mental upkeep. We assume our minds are jogging along just fine. We forget that every bit of information we are taking in each second of the day is affecting the way our minds work and how efficiently they run.

Maybe you spend hours on social media every day although you know deep down that it makes you feel a bit shit. Here is a classic example of how we can get confused as to who is running the show. The whole body, mind and magic may feel dulled and diluted with this activity, but we tell ourselves: 'This is just what you do every day, get over it.' Make a change. Stop looking at something that makes you feel bad. Put the phone down. Get your mind and body feeling good. Tell that brain what to do.

Maybe you're in a relationship that is unfulfilling. Your whole self feels slightly downtrodden and like you're coasting, but your mind is telling you that you probably won't find anyone else. It whispers to you that this is just how your life is and that you don't deserve any better. It will come up with thousands of reasons why you should stay so you ignore that whole body, mind and inner gut sensation of wanting out. Get back in the driving seat. Tell your mind to think with clarity. Ask it to work with your body and soul to source out the best it can and to allow you to know what you want and feel you truly deserve. Don't let your mind's worry and fear take over.

REST YOUR MIND

Getting your head in good shape requires daily practice. You can flex that muscle in whichever way feels good, as it has to feel right for you. The hurdle is getting your mind to stop. To give it rest outside of when you're sleeping. It needs to recharge and go blank for some much-needed breathing space and clarity. We cannot make good decisions when all the cogs are turning with thousands of ideas, thoughts and concerns. It needs to deflate and bliss out for a bit so it can then work to its optimum when you really need it to.

Yoga works well for me (have a flick through the Happy Body section of this book), as it makes my mind concentrate only on what my body is doing. It goes with the breath and I relax into each pose without thought or judgement. After I've done yoga I often have clear ideas and thoughts that make a difference to my day.

Meditation is another excellent way of achieving that brain Zen. I find this much more difficult and often procrastinate while trying to follow this well-trodden and celebrated path. I know it works, but I still don't do it enough to really benefit me. The one time I was very disciplined about it was when I was pregnant. I found I was much kinder to myself and more pragmatic when I was pregnant, as I was focusing more on the baby. Meditating made me feel that I could truly rest my mind and body, so the baby would feel calm and at peace with the whole process. I meditated every day before bed and it helped me have a relaxed pregnancy first time around, and also helped with my severe sickness the second time around. If the thought of sitting cross-legged on the floor while attempting to battle hundreds of thoughts that keep creeping into your mind does not appeal, there is a guided meditation coming up from my friend Hollie.

HELLO TO . . . HOLLIE

Hollie is another amazing person who I was lucky enough to have met through friends. A mate of mine, Giovanna, had experienced a calm and relaxed birth, which fascinated me as my first birth with my son Rex was long, intense and not relaxing in the slightest. I couldn't believe it was possible and quizzed her further.

Giovanna had met with Hollie De Cruz, a hypnobirthing expert, to learn the magic of her theories. When I found out I was pregnant with my second child, Honey, I knew I had to give it a try. The first time I met with Hollie she took me through some guided meditations to help me through the extreme nine-month-long morning sickness I was plodding through. Her visualisations gave me a chance to escape the twenty-four-hour sickness on some level, as my mind was taken to other places. At this point I could see how powerful this hypnotherapy could be and how I could use it in labour.

When I applied Hollie's mediations and visualisations during the birth of Honey, I felt so much calmer than I had with my son, Rex. Hollie emailed me some guided meditations that I listened to most nights while pregnant and then when I was giving birth to Honey. My mind felt stronger and gave my body the confidence to get through it without fear. My labour was calm, mostly relaxed and incredible, as I realised what my body was capable of.

I still use Hollie's MP3's to help get to sleep at night or to take five minutes out if I'm on the train to work. The power of visualisation is a game-changer. You can use it to get your mind on track to wherever you want to be.

The guided meditation that follows is a great form of escapism if you're feeling overwhelmed or stressed. Read it over a couple of times so you roughly know the story of it in your head. If you're lucky, you could even ask your partner or friend to read it aloud whilst you close your eyes and shut off. Then relax and go through the suggested places and sensations. Focus on your breath and the pictures in your imagination, and give your mind a break.

HOLLIE: So just close your eyes, and before you begin to relax, take a moment to make yourself comfortable, and feel free to change position at any time if you need to. Begin now to tune in with your own breath, and on an exhale that feels good for you, let your shoulders soften and give yourself permission to relax.

Breathe fully, and breathe deeply. Inhaling peace, and exhaling tension. Let the breath flow all the way down through your chest and your stomach. Let it drift all the way down your legs until you feel the soft tingling of relaxation reach the soles of your feet.

Return your attention now to your eyes – feel how comfortable they have become, and feel now that relaxation spread all across your forehead and your temples. Feel all the little worry lines just fade and disappear, and if you are holding a frown, just easily release it and notice how good that feels. And now feel that wonderful deep relaxation spread on down over your nose and your cheeks, all the way down to your mouth and your jaw. Take a moment to place your tongue behind your upper teeth, and allow your lower jaw to recede, as you drift deeper, and still deeper into this wonderful state of calm relaxation.

With every breath, you allow yourself to relax even more deeply, and on your next exhale, just let your shoulders gently sink into the frame of your body, and feel how relaxed and limp they have become. Your body feels entirely relaxed and at ease, and you feel all tension and worry just drifting away.

And now in your mind's eye, and your imagination, I want you to visualise a beautiful blue sky, and take yourself to your favourite spot in nature. This could be a place from your childhood, a spot that you are fond of now, or perhaps even a place that only exists in your imagination. See yourself here. This is a place where you feel totally safe and secure. A place where there is no tension or worry. A place where you can enjoy the wonderful feeling of being yourself. So safe and secure.

Look around you, take in all of the things around you. Notice what you are standing on – perhaps it is dry grass, or maybe warm sand – notice what this feels like on your bare feet. Be aware of the sounds around you too. Maybe you can hear birds singing, or trees blowing gently in the breeze, or maybe the sound of water trickling down a stream, or the sea gently lapping up against the shore. These sounds make you feel calm, connected and at peace. They make you feel safe. I want you to notice now what the warmth of the sun feels like on your skin. Maybe you can feel its warm golden glow just softly soothing every part of you.

And now, as you visualise the numbers from ten down to one, I want you to feel that warmth just gradually drifting down your body, allowing you to go deeper and deeper into this wonderful state of calmness and relaxation.

So beginning to count now. Ten ... you can feel that warmth wash down over your head and face, nine... feeling the light spread into your neck and your shoulders as they gently relax, eight ... and all the way down your arms, allowing your elbows to feel relaxed and limp, seven ... feeling this calming energy flow into your hands, and all the way into your fingertips as they gently rest in your lap or by your sides, six ... letting that golden light down through your chest and your stomach, five ... breathing light and love down to your very core, four ... feeling the warmth softly relax your pelvis and all around your hips, releasing all tension, three ... light travelling down the tops of your legs and all around your knees, two ... feeling that soft tingling sensation of relaxation reaching the soles of your feet and the tips of your toes, and one ... feeling completely and wonderfully relaxed, free of all cares and worries, happy and peaceful.

You may continue to rest here, enjoying the wonderful sense of relaxation that softly penetrates every part of you, and knowing that you can access this place of quiet whenever you need to.

Remember that all you need to do to achieve this sense of peace and calmness is to make yourself comfortable and tune in to your own breath – inhaling peace and exhaling tension. As you do, you'll begin to let go and continue to drift into this place of deep relaxation. Each time you practise, it becomes easier and easier to reach this deeply relaxed state.

So now, continue to rest, to breathe, to relax – allowing your mind and your body to take the break they deserve. Know that right now, nobody wants anything – nobody needs anything – there is absolutely nothing to do but relax and let go.

Learning to relax like this will manifest into your ordinary everyday life, and you will enjoy this wonderful new sense of calmness and confidence. You will find it so easy to cope with the stresses and strains of everyday life, because you now know how to relax, and you can access your new skill whenever you need to.

Now I want you to count from one up to five. When you reach five you will open your eyes and bring your awareness back to the room, feeling mentally alert, physically energised, and emotionally calm and confident.

,,

FIND A CREATIVE RITUAL

If meditation doesn't do it for you, maybe you know an activity that allows your brain to have that vacation moment. Whatever your chosen activity, make it something in your life that allows you to have mental space where you shut off. Even walking and focusing on your every footstep rather than looking at your phone for the whole journey can help you zone out.

Art, for me, has always been a go-to extra-curricular way to get the balance back. It takes me home, makes me remember what I'm really about and calms every cell in my body. Each time, it's a journey that takes me through many emotions subconsciously. I start feeling nervous that the painting won't turn out how I want and then excited as it takes shape. I then go off on tangents of feeling thrilled and buzzed, to feeling annoyed if mistakes are made. The end result, however, always remains the same. Sheer bliss. It's a calm that settles after I've signed my name at the bottom of the canvas. I've created something. Whether others appreciate what I've made or have emotions attached to my work is irrelevant at this point. The process and magical flow that I experienced, for those minutes or hours, is what has nourished my soul.

I don't think you have to be good at painting to grab hold of

this feeling. Putting pen or brush to paper releases all sorts of hypnotic qualities that leap forward once you open your mind. The freedom of art is to be explored and taken advantage of.

NO RULES

I paint what I see with exaggerated touches that feel important to me. If I'm painting faces (my favourite subject), I often enlarge the eyes as I feel they're the doorway to our souls. They tell stories even though a silent painting can't, and show how the person in the frame is really feeling. I may accentuate bright gleaming light on the hair and forehead and leave thick brush strokes on purpose to draw your attention to how the light fell that day. I may create harsher angles than needed if the person I'm painting feels more masculine than feminine.

A great friend of mine, Mr Gok Wan, who is equally passionate about painting, has a completely different style. He flexes his artistic muscles by smearing colourful globs of Japanese ink over a bright white canvas with plastic paddles. It creates a delicious scene of chaos and colour with a hidden message and story. It's there for you to find in your own time. There are no rules. Your own emotional state and frame of mind will set the scene for how your pictures should take place and then your ideas around the piece can be explained or left as a mystery when finished.

One of my favourite artists is Jonathan Yeo, who keeps parts of his giant canvases sketchy and worn so chunks of his very accurate and delicate work on a face will fade to the unknown. His visions of certain well-known faces are left slightly unfinished so you can make up the rest of the story yourself – like we all do when we meet someone in real life. This for me says so much, as we never really know a person 100 per cent, even when we think we do.

When I'm mid-painting, and I've managed to push through the initial desire to procrastinate, I feel numb. Not the kind of numb where you feel lifeless and grey but the sort where time is suspended, physical wants dissipate into the canvas and thoughts halt for endless ticking seconds. BLISS! I feel lucky to have found my creative flow and that it lives at the end of a paint brush.

When I was pregnant, Hollie told me to **visualise** a coloured balloon when in labour. She asked me to pick a colour and I instinctively said purple. All through my labour, I visualised this balloon with clarity – recognising its shape, texture and colour. This visual helped me massively in more intense moments and gave me a clear **focus**. I love to use colours for visualisations.

Write down a situation that is causing you stress or sadness:

Pick a colour that seems to represent this situation. Colour in this box with that colour.

Now pick a colour that represents happy to you, and colour this box in with that colour.

Imagine breathing in **great sweeps** of your happy colour and let it swamp your lungs. Now breathe out the colour that represents your stress and pain. Exhale a huge stream of this colour and watch it leave your body and drift away. Then repeat by inhaling your beautiful **happy** tone and exhale the negative colour. Do this for as long as you need. It'll help to get your heart rate down and allows you to release some of the physical tension that you've built up.

SOME CREATIVE IDEAS

 Creative flow is so important and doesn't have to be too planned or over-thought. I haven't had much time to paint since my children were born so I've channeled my creative flow into baking and cooking. This sort of creative flow has the added benefit of edible results for all to enjoy! Cooking can be a practical hobby that requires little fanfare but gives huge amounts of head space and joy during and after. There's something so cathartic about grating a carrot or whisking an egg, a simple physical action that triggers the brain to quieten down and remain static while this polite ritual occurs. Concentrating on timings, temperatures, textures and the alchemy of flavour combination all create this dream-like physical and mental state for me. I feel lucky to have stumbled across this hobby along the way.

My husband says playing the guitar for him opens up this same portal of good vibes and allows him to escape previously held-onto worries that then bleed into insignificance while the chords flow. Being skilled at playing an instrument is a creative outlet that takes time and practice, but once you nail it you can switch off mentally and enjoy what your muscles and mind have retained through repetition. I envy this skill my husband so naturally has.

Simple moments in life can be injected with a shot of **grandeur** and importance by turning them into **rituals**. For me this is making my morning coffee. I love this daily ritual and take my time in enjoying each step of making it. I sip each inch of the hot rich liquid and am grateful for the flavour and warmth. It's a non-moveable daily practice that gives me vast amounts of **joy**. These tiny moments can become important, as you to take the time to notice the wonder around you. Maybe its your walk to work in the morning, or getting dressed and ready for the day.

Write down a ritual for **yourself** here. Take time daily to love every millisecond of its magic

My ritual is:

. . . .

I love it because:

. . . .

. . . .

. . . .

. . . .

. . . .

. . . .

Even doodling can have a great effect on the mind, as you sub-consciously pour your inner thoughts onto a scrap of paper and let those thoughts live and breathe outside your mind. It can be therapeutic and joyful ,as you let go and create something new at the same time. It's such a simple way of switching off while simultaneously getting in touch with what is really going on inside.

Whatever your creative outlet is, do it often, do it with joy and feel the bliss.

Here's some space to **doodle** . . .

A COUPLE OF
HAPPY RECIPES

I love to cook and even if I'm in a rush (with the kids hungrily running around the kitchen), I try to note its importance and ritualistic tendencies. Grating, chopping, stirring and arranging. Each step of the process quietens my brain and brings a peaceful air to the general chaos of life. If you haven't found a ritual yet, then borrow mine! Here are two healthy recipes for you to try. They involve grating and chopping, which should allow you some time and space away from the madness to zone out, and then enjoy.

CHOPPED
SALAD

This is a crisp, light and fresh salad that offers up a load of flavour and crunch. I find it's a quick yet therapeutic recipe to make. I love the process of chopping all the veg and apple and then combining all of those crisp flavours. The dressing is creamy and luxurious but still light and easy to digest. A year-round salad champ.

2 apples, cored and
    roughly chopped
100g radishes, roughly
    chopped
150g cucumber, roughly
    chopped
150g cooked quinoa
150g lettuce, chopped
200g feta, crumbled
80g goji berries
Smalla handful of fresh
    flat-leaf parsley
    leaves, roughly
    chopped
Small handful of fresh
    mint leaves, roughly
    chopped
100g walnuts, roasted
1 tsp sumac, for
    sprinkling (optional)

FOR THE YOGHURT DRESSING:

100g yoghurt (Greek,
    soy or coconut)
1 garlic clove, crushed
Grated zest of 1 lemon,
    and juice of half
3 tbsp extra-virgin
    olive oil
Sea salt and freshly
    ground black pepper

4    **5**

SERVES 4

For the dressing, combine the yoghurt, garlic, lemon zest, and most of the lemon juice and olive oil in a bowl. Season to taste with salt and pepper. Cover and set aside.

For the salad, combine the chopped apples, radishes, cucumber, cooked quinoa, lettuce and most of the feta, goji berries, herbs and walnuts in a bowl. Drizzle over the remaining lemon juice and olive oil, season with a little salt, pepper and sumac (if using) and toss to combine.

Plate up the salad on a large serving dish, drizzle over the yoghurt dressing, then scatter over the remaining feta, goji berries, herbs and walnuts.

COURGETTE AND CARROT FRITTERS

For some reason I get great pleasure from grating. Any monotonous actions during cooking send my head into a clearer and more rested place. This is a wonderfully quick dinner that looks impressive but takes very little time to prepare. Cook up a batch if you have friends over for dinner and serve on a sharing plate, or fry up as many as desired and store the rest of the mixture in the fridge for up to a couple of days. They're full of flavour and feel very hearty as they're packed with veg. These are a firm favourite in our house.

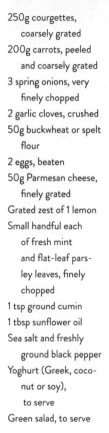

250g courgettes, coarsely grated

200g carrots, peeled and coarsely grated

3 spring onions, very finely chopped

2 garlic cloves, crushed

50g buckwheat or spelt flour

2 eggs, beaten

50g Parmesan cheese, finely grated

Grated zest of 1 lemon

Small handful each of fresh mint and flat-leaf parsley leaves, finely chopped

1 tsp ground cumin

1 tbsp sunflower oil

Sea salt and freshly ground black pepper

Yoghurt (Greek, coconut or soy), to serve

Green salad, to serve

MAKES 16 SMALL FRITTERS, TO SERVE 4–6

Spread the grated courgettes and carrots out on a board, and sprinkle over a teaspoon of salt. Set aside for ten minutes.

Meanwhile, combine the spring onions, garlic, flour, eggs, Parmesan, lemon zest, most of the herbs and the cumin in a large bowl.

Place the courgettes and carrots in a clean tea towel and squeeze out as much liquid as possible. Add the vegetables to the bowl and mix together until thoroughly combined.

Heat the sunflower oil in a deep frying pan over a medium heat. Once hot, place one heaped tablespoon of the courgette mix for each fritter, flattening out gently to form a rough round shape. I can usually get about four in at one time. Fry for 2–3 minutes on each side until crisp and golden. Transfer to a plate and keep warm while you continue with the rest.

To serve, plate up the fritters with the remaining herbs scattered over. Serve immediately with a dollop of yoghurt and a green salad.

ANXIETY AND THE
RULEBOOK

Now I'm going to talk about something that seems to be affecting more and more people lately: anxiety. Anxiety is my most frequent kill joy. That lurking feeling that something is not quite right, that snowballs quickly into panic. The lines between feeling a bit anxious and having anxiety proper can be blurred, but there is definitely a difference. My own experience of anxiety has luckily never reached the extremes where it's been a huge problem but is something I know I still need to work on. Having severe anxiety issues is of course a weighty matter that can hinder you in everyday life. When worry and fear are frequently in the driving seat and your life feels like a series of huge and scary hurdles each and every second, then make sure you look for help. The Mind website has a lot of information on this subject and even a helpline to call.

Small drops of anxiety first made an appearance on the scene when I started to venture outside of the small and comfy world I had grown up in. As I moved away from the things, places and people I knew, I started to experience anxiety about how others saw me. Had I unintentionally upset someone, or said something that made someone wince? Or misjudged a scenario? My brain would spin out as I dissected moments and conversations gone by. I still have this creeping dread socially from time to time, but the older I get and the more comfortable I am in my own skin, the less I worry about it all. I'm not sure if this just comes with time or is strengthened through the experiences life throws your way. I think when you get into the groove of knowing it's okay just to be YOU, things get easier.

These days my anxiety stems from breaking those rules I have created for myself. It could be a moment I'm worried about in the future, a past event that still has its claws in me or something tiny that has the potential to grow into a monster. For instance, I may be out with my young children and realise it's edging towards their bedtime. I can hear the clock ticking quickly and loudly as I feel anxiety swirl around my chest. What will happen if I don't get them back in time? Absolutely nothing. But because I've created a set of rules that feel comfy, I get a very edgy feeling that something might go 'wrong', and feel discomfort about this abnormal territory and the fear of the unknown. If I can stop the process in time and remind myself that the fast-approaching bedtime is just a marker I have created, then I can get back to a place of calm.

Sometimes I will feel anxious stepping into a very busy environment, as again I've created a rule that states I prefer the calm. This gets in the way of me experiencing something new with an open mind. I get caught up in my own story and can't melt into the moment with fresh eyes; instead I bring along my date for the night, anxiety. My antisocial date clings onto my arm, morphing my body language into a stiffened state, and stops my mouth from moving in the desired way.

In my bespoke rulebook, I've also set standards and expectations that I expect myself to rise to. If I don't meet these goals I find myself gathering that anxious momentum yet again.

Many times I have looked around me at others who are seemingly in control and not led by fear and their own rules. They seem so carefree and relaxed in their own achievements, or lack of. I too have many glorious sunny times where I relax into what's going on around me with abandon and it feels great, but I find it tough to harness that bliss all of the time. Anxiety is the main perpetrator in defeating this joy. The edgy, lurking feeling that something isn't quite right even when you look around and can't see any danger at all.

It's not until I remember to tear up my own rulebook that I can let go and welcome new and exciting possibilities. I can move the goalposts and I can create my own boundaries to work with. That in itself makes future anxiety that bit easier to dilute.

If I do begin to panic in situations such as these, then I try to remember that it can be extinguished if I act from a calm place. This is much easier said than done at times, but I think having the awareness that you know you feel a little freaked out is a great start. Then you can take some deep breaths and get back to knowing that you'll be okay if you slow that heart rate down and act from a place of calm.

NEVER BE AFRAID TO ASK FOR HELP

When I know I have slipped into the abyss of anxiety, I have to speak to someone. Just as it is one of my key tools when I find myself in the black, talking is my way out. If I'm feeling down I know I can go for a walk, listen to music, paint or watch something joyful to help lift me but anxiety, for me, cannot be tamed alone. I need a calm and strong-minded outside source to talk me out of where I've ended up.

I feel lucky to have great friends and family members I can call upon in these times, whose softly spoken words and grounded philosophies will douse the anxiety with a bucket full of calm. I also have many friends who will come to me to have their own anxieties tamed and calmed. Sharing is key.

Asking for help used to be excruciating but now I take great comfort in using someone else's words and theories to climb out of a ditch. Seeking support can make you feel vulnerable, but people who love you will only meet that openness with love and empathy. I now get great pleasure in calling a dear friend, spilling out my panic in a speedy torrent and feeling an instant relief as it's out of my head and cradled by another. Never be afraid to ask for help. It's the gateway to new ways of thinking and new paths, as energies shift.

Anxiety is so much more prevalent these days, as there's so much pressure on us all to be everything. We don't give ourselves a break and we leave no room for mistakes. I'm a classic case of someone who hates to let mistakes in. I see mistakes as failures that leave me a lesser version of myself, and somehow 'damaged goods'. Instead, we all need to understand what we can learn from those moments where everything is seemingly going 'wrong'.

If we can all learn to knock down the high expectations we have of ourselves and give ourselves a break, this anxiety has less to feed off. If we can take a step back from our own rulebooks and the way we think things should be, there's more space in our minds and lives, and we achieve an expanded vision of everything going on around us.

BEDTIME DIARY

I find it hard to get enough sleep with an irregular work schedule and young children. After nights I've worked late, my kids seem to hone into this sleep deprivation and wake even earlier the next day. I'm never on the ball when I'm deprived of sleep and have a shorter temper and less empathy for others. It's hard to take naps in the day with so much going on but I'll always endeavour to get more sleep the following night if I can. Keep a log of how many hours you're getting per night; if it's less than eight, see if you can pull it back by the end of the week. Good Luck!

MON

TUE

WED

THU

FRI

SAT

SUN

Writing proves massively cathartic for me. I love to let my mind wander, which in turn leads to releasing all sorts of undiscovered emotions and feelings. See what happens when you give yourself a blank page and a pen. Let your mind wander by finishing off this short story.

The night was dark and the stars were bright . . .

ACCEPT YOURSELF, WARTS AND ALL

Luckily I have many anxiety-free, joyful moments, where I look back and view the more frantic and panicky times like they were happening to someone else. When the storm of worry has passed, my perspective seems much clearer and more grounded. Sometimes I look back and feel embarrassed or even concerned as to how I got myself in such a state about something so small. Sometimes I can almost laugh, but not quite, as I know at the time the anxiety had control over me and that's something that makes me feel a bit sad. I feel I've wasted possible golden moments in life by travelling so far from what I actually believe. I have got so lost, away from 'home'; that place that is real and that I know to be true.

What I need to do is learn to view these moments as knots in a piece of wood. Twisted, possibly unattractive and uncomfortable, but a part of me. I've spoken about it a lot already, but I guess acceptance is the key. I need to look back and accept that I am not a perfect human being who always thinks positively and acts from a happy place and that's okay. There is room for it all.

EMBRACE THE GOOD TIMES

 Enjoying the great times is crucial. There lies the balance of life. Acknowledging and accepting that there will always be good and bad, and that it's how we deal with it all that counts. When anxiety is nowhere to be seen I feel very in the moment, something I've improved at over the years. I can sit and zone out by looking at a breathtaking view or beautiful sky for several minutes, soaking up every delicious second. It's one of my favourite things to do. I truly know in these snatches of time that I am okay and that I am viewing and absorbing all the beauty around me. Gratitude seeps subconsciously from every pore during these timeless moments and anxiety has no room to breathe.

Recently I lay on the patio in the garden and looked up at the stars twinkling in the black velvet sky above. Just stopping for half an hour to take a proper look at the constellations – and their constant reminder of how small we are – was enough to get me feeling in the moment and truly in wonder at everything around me. I look out of the window most nights, but never bother to stop and take it all in. This patio session shifted my whole perspective on tiny worries and concerns, as I felt like a small speck of dust floating about among these giant balls of light.

Laughter is the next easily glugged tonic for me. It snaps me back into my body and dulls the anxiety to a much quieter and more distant hum. Just recently I fell into a fit of giggles in a yoga class when my husband performed the most glorious clumsy fall. Knowing those around me were in their own bubble of serenity only tipped me further into a body-shaking episode of laughter. BLISS! Naughty, as the timing was bad, but so so fun. Listening to a funny podcast or watching a brilliant film can be equally powerful, as you step away from that lurking feeling of dread and focus on letting go with roars of laughter.

Music is one of the most powerful game-changers in my life. It can throw me back to another time in a split second, as I recall smells, tastes and emotions from another chunk of my life. New music has an equally intoxicating quality, as your ears pull out sounds that lull you into a safe place of harmonies and lyrics that mean something to you, even though you've never heard them before.

Music for me will always be a go-to for moving through situations and grabbing hold of the next chapter. Sometimes these songs will be relaxing as my mind craves static, chilled-out songs that will soothe my exhausted head into a hazy state of calm. At other times I'll need upbeat, soaring tunes that feel like they're pushing the anxiety away. The sheer force of their brilliance and beats will move the pain and stress to another realm as my body and mind start to work with other emotions connected to the music. There are no rules; the songs will find you.

Whatever your feel-good needs are, make sure you find them and go with it. Be in the moment, lean in to the good times and stare at the stars.

THINK POSITIVE

As I talked about in HAPPY CHOICES, when we are met with a situation in life, fundamentally we choose to either act from a place of fear or a place of love. A positive or a negative. When we're making a decision from a positive place, our whole body reacts before our mind gets a chance to interfere with its judgement, worry and doubt.

As I know how delicate my own mind can be, I try to steer away from unnecessary negativity when I can. I don't watch scary or violent films and I don't go on websites that only feature negative gossip. It doesn't make me feel all-round good. It will spark something in my head that could send me off in a direction I don't want. I need to be fuelled by positivity whenever possible.

Inevitably, negative stories or situations will crop up, but if I can control the ones in my day-to-day life on a smaller level, then I will do that. I like to read books that feel inspiring, watch films that feed

Here is my happy playlist. These songs all boost my mood, have the power to move negative energy on and give me a twinkle in my eye. I have this list on my Spotify account fearnecottonofficial, so if you like these songs come give it a listen!

HAPPY PLAYLIST

'ROCKET MAN' – *Elton John*

This song, from start to finish, makes every cell in my body come alive. It takes me back to a bar in a tent at Glastonbury where my husband and I sang loudly; it takes me back to my labours, as it was on my birthing playlist – and both labours, although intense, were the most euphoric moments of my existence. It takes me back to late and very funny nights in Las Vegas with a group of great mates.

There's something about how the verse builds and then explodes into this harmonious chorus. Spine tingling!

'ALL YOU NEED IS LOVE' – *The Beatles*

The best feel-good sing-along song ever. It's near impossible to keep yourself from mouthing these lyrics very passionately. Just one listen lightens the load and makes your eyes sparkle. At the end of the day, it is all about love!

'RAMBLE ON' – *Led Zeppelin*

This track moves stuff on. It has the rhythm and power to shift energy and get you through tough times. Robert Plant sings these lyrics with such urgency that you can tell how much of a release it is for him. You can only draw on this and expel your own negativity. Play this loud!

'FANS' – *Kings of Leon*

As soon as this song starts, the sun starts to shine somewhere. I've spent many a rainy London afternoon listening to this, letting it take my head to a far-off sunny place. It gets your feet tapping, your head nodding and the corners of your mouth lifting!

'10,000 EMERALD POOLS'
– *Børns*

This song mellows your whole body and soul in one swoop. Its laid-back tempo and angelic vocals are like a cool summer breeze. I always start moving at half the speed when this is playing, and I switch from racing around to swaying with a smile. Blissful.

'40 DAY DREAM' – *Edward Sharpe and the Magnetic Zeros*

This band are the masters of creating a party atmosphere at their gigs, where everyone sings and dances and gets to know their neighbour. This song is a perfect example of how they go about their business. It's one big happy family singalong.

'TRENCH TOWN ROCK'
– *Bob Marley*

Telling the story of the power of music so perfectly. This atmospheric song says it all!

'MYKONOS' – *Fleet Foxes*

The musical equivalent of a mojito, this song makes me sink into my chair and breathe a sigh of relief. It's joyful and relaxing and an all-round ball of bliss.

'PHENOMENAL WOMAN'
– *Laura Mvula*

Everything about this lady's voice is the dream. She is my all-encompassing female power hero. This song is high-energy happiness.

'I GOT U' – *Duke Dumont*

Even if you didn't hear this on holiday, you will feel nostalgic for the last beach you visited when this songs plays. It makes me feel hopeful and excited for what lies ahead.

'LOUD PLACES' – *Jamie XX*

This song is more of an atmosphere than anything else. It makes everything around you come alive and has such a happy cinematic quality. It's soft but upbeat at the same time, which is the perfect balance.

'OOH LA LA' – *The Faces*

This is a request by my stepchildren, who adore this song. Seeing them sing along to it with huge smiles is enough to make me beam from ear to ear.

'MMMBOP' – *Hanson*

This throws me straight back to being a teenager without a care in the world. The summers seemed longer and hotter and are most definitely rose-tinted, but that's the beauty of being transported back in time with music.

'SIGNED, SEALED, DELIVERED' – *Stevie Wonder*

Any note Stevie sings is pumped and fuelled with joy. You can tell he is smiling when he is singing this, which only makes it that bit more infectious. Happiness, note by note.

'COOL' – *Le Youth*

This is another summer-coated song that makes me feel warmer from the second it starts. Most songs that remind me of the summer infuse me with feel-good vibes; this is most definitely one of them.

'9 TO 5' – *Dolly Parton*

I had to include this, as I adore Dolly, and it's impossible not to dance to this song. It's an all-round crowd-pleaser when I DJ and I will never ever get bored of it.

my brain with either laughter or stories I can learn from. I want to surround myself with people who talk from the heart and are as willing to share their story as I am mine. These are the parts of my life I feel I have control over and the ones I can make a choice about. They are all changeable parts of your life, too.

It's strange that the negative is usually so much louder than the positive. It shouts from above in a gravelly, alarming tone and seems much bigger than any positive nearby. Positivity seems to have a gentle whisper that can get overlooked or taken for granted. But that's because it doesn't need to shout or stomp about. It is self-assured and grounded.

YOUR MIND CAN CHANGE

We know the brain has the capacity to change as we look back on our own lives. We can adapt and change our habits and thought processes, whenever we want to – a liberating epiphany that I regularly stumble upon. Aha! I can change. Freedom!

Once we recognise this, we can start to steer our lives in whatever direction we desire. We all fundamentally want joy and happiness in our lives, so if that's the foundation of all of our life choices then it makes decision-making that bit easier. We can use our minds to seek out the positive and joyful in each moment and to gravitate towards people and activities that feel good.

I have found that when I get into a habit of thinking in this way, I naturally see more positivity. It seems to spring up out of the blue and is much more prevalent all round. If you go to the gym for a few months, you'll find that the exercises you found tough on week one are now much easier and feel more natural to you. It's the same with how we train our brains to think. After a while, grabbing hold of the plusses in life doesn't feel like such an effort, and you seem to seek them out more frequently and with ease.

THE RIPPLES OF YOUR HAPPY MIND

Keeping in good mental shape is a necessity, not only for me but for my family. I want to be in the best headspace possible for my children and my husband, so we can continue having fun and raising our kids in a way that feels good to us.

When I'm in a good space mentally, I can spread my own good feelings to others and let it ripple out to unknown places. I'll smile at a stranger on the street, and maybe this will give them a little positive boost that they then pass on through their actions to those around them. This will in turn ripple out to all the people's lives around THEM and help to keep those feel-good vibrations moving on across the planet. It doesn't take much. Just one little moment or gesture. It all helps the bigger picture. So get your mind in good shape, remember it's a daily exercise, and let your own feel-good magic spread as far as it can.

Summary

TAKE CHARGE OF YOUR MIND.

You're in control of it. Don't let your habits or fears run the show.

REST YOUR MIND.

Give it space to breathe and find creative outlets to help slow down the cogs.

YOU CAN CHANGE.

Freedom! You're writing your own story – don't ever feel confined.

WHAT DOES HAPPY **MIND**
LOOK LIKE TO YOU?

Write one word or draw a picture here that sums it up

HAPPY *Body*

This chapter is not about weight loss, toned abs or faddy diets. It's about love, respect and gratitude. My relationship with my own body has changed massively over the years and has morphed from one of anguish, destruction and abuse to one of love, comfort and thanks – a much happier place to be.

I LOVE my body. I'm not talking about an aesthetic love where I spend hours adoring my calves in a mirror, I'm talking about viewing my body as a miraculous machine that can self-heal, create and move. A happy body to me is one that feels comfortable. One that is fuelled in a balanced way, rested when possible and one that is enjoyed rather than criticised.

HAPPY BODY = HAPPY MIND

It may seem obvious to mention that our bodies and minds work together and have a vital and strong alliance, but I think stopping to take note of this makes us feel slightly more in control. With the gargantuan power our minds have the ability to apply, combined with the strength of the human body, we can do so much, or very little. And it goes both ways, by looking after our bodies, our minds can feel the equilibrium so essential to feeling happy and calm.

Our bodies have to work in tandem with our minds and I think we might have slightly lost this connection over the years. These days we see our bodies as a separate and tangible portion of our makeup, while our minds fling about elsewhere, unrelated and without consequence. We exercise in the gym to get a better body and eat food to fuel it; while we go to school to flex our brain, and watch TV or read books to zone out. Rarely do we think of the two as a vital partnership that needs to run at the same speed and with the same goal in mind.

In my twenties my goal used to be to achieve: run at a faster speed, work more, feel excited and to push my own boundaries. My old ways and thoughts seem a vast canyon away from today's priorities. In that huge space lie a lot of mistakes and mental and physical upheaval but, on the upside, all that took place in that time has led me to my new set of life rules and tools.

I now aim, both mentally and physically, for a lack of adrenalin, a peace and a balance that I would have previously found 'boring'. Personally, what works for me is having calm in my mind and my body so it can grow and function and heal as needed. It means that I now sleep deeper and can deal with lack of sleep (due to my gorgeous children!) a lot better. I have much more energy as I pay attention to what goes into my body, and feel much happier in my own skin. Mentally I am boosted and deal with stress a lot better if I'm in a calm place. I also don't feel led by my mind as much anymore, as my thoughts and stress levels aren't steering the ship so often. Some days, I can calm my physical side with good thoughts and a positive mindset but equally I can quieten my mind with slow and considered physical movements. Body and mind can work alongside each other and also help each other out.

LISTEN TO YOUR BODY

I constantly think back to my teens and twenties, when I had little regard for my body and all that it was miraculously doing. I would work on many filming projects at the same time, rushing from location to location, at times flying in and out of time zones with no days off to rest. I didn't see the point, as those rest periods seemed like obstacles in this race to get me to where I wanted to be. I would eat on the run and not care if the food was good fuel (I'm talking a bag of sweets and a strong coffee for breakfast), and would work and move until I was physically exhausted. I made choices that I simply would not make now. During this time I partied until late without much sleep and I put little energy into thinking about what fuel my body needed. Mentally, I chased emotional highs and was always seeking adventure regardless of the outcome.

I made these decisions and my body suffered as a result. I was constantly exhausted, had a greyish tinge to my skin and felt slightly on edge a lot of the time. Although I think that naturally I would have grown tired of this fast-paced way of living, this chapter ended more suddenly, in an implosion of depression and physical stress that eventually led me down this wonderful new path of seeking happiness.

Being a teenager or twenty-something is a great time for pushing boundaries, experimenting with what works for you and having immense fun, as long as you listen to your inner compass telling you when you've pushed it too far. I don't regret the lack of sleep, or feeling overwhelmed when I worked too much, I just wish I had listened to my instincts a bit more during this decade, as this could have saved me a lot of stress. I could have eaten better and helped my energy levels, and also respected my body's strength and health a lot more than I did. However, these are all lessons I learned in good time. One life chapter has to come to a close for a new one to begin. This shift could be a slow realisation that things might need to change or, like in my case, a quick cold shock, but whichever way it happens, you'll learn as you go and find new comfort in where you end up.

I still seek physical and mental adventure these days, but from a place of calm. I can feel the spectrum of all-round emotion but from a place where I'm aware of the outcome it will have on my whole being.

BEST MATES

I now crave calm, peace and balance throughout. My mind and body have to be mates, BEST mates, that work alongside each other and warn each other if one side feels slightly weaker than the other. I can't expect to have a great night's sleep physically if my mind is racing at 100 miles per hour. I can't expect to get out of a dark hole emotionally if I've been drinking lots of gin and not eating properly. Why do we expect so much of our bodies without regard to what's going on upstairs? I often lie in bed at night after I've finished a long exciting evening of filming and am met by a hard wall of insomnia. I have experienced this for the past twenty years of my career, but still get wound up and irritated that I can't sleep. Recently I've tried listening to peaceful music on my way home from work or a guided meditation (see page 130) to try to take the edge off the adrenalin. If I don't do this, I'll have a shitty night's sleep, wake early with the kids and most definitely feel slightly bedraggled the next day. I have to put that bit more effort into moving from exciting work mode back to grounded ready-for-bed mode.

Let's face it, strain is unavoidable in life. Many people have physically demanding jobs which can take their toll. Even being a parent is demanding on the body, from pregnancy through to carrying babies on hips, rushing around after everyone but yourself and eating quickly and irregularly. Maybe your job involves a lot of sitting, like my shifts at Radio 1 – I always felt stiff and physically lifeless after a long day in my radio chair, and felt like I needed to walk for miles to inject some energy back into my joints. Life can never be plotted out in a dream sequence but there are ways we can give ourselves a helping hand . . .

BE NICE TO YOURSELF

It all starts with gratitude for our bodies, something I had very little of growing up. Now I am in awe of the human body. It is an incredible machine that is unrivalled by any invention. It can self-heal, grow, change, move and create, but we have to love it first.

There is a sweet experiment I saw online, started by Nikki Owen, where a mum and her young son put two apples on two separate dishes, and each day they would go to Apple A and say something like: 'You are a wonderful apple, look at your shiny green skin and beautiful spherical shape. Oh we love you darling apple.'

Then they would walk to Apple B and say something like: 'AND look at you! So ugly and bulbous. You are the worst apple I've ever laid eyes on. How dare you call yourself an apple, you gross monster of a fruit.'

Apple A remained a beautifully shiny green fruit for some weeks, whereas Apple B crinkled and rotted more quickly than you would believe.

What we can draw from this is that everything around us picks up on our energy, good or bad. Our words and thoughts are powerful and not to be underestimated. Used in the right way, words can do wonders. How do you talk to your body? Is it Apple A or B? We've all been known to slam ourselves and attach shame to our physical form, but if you start with humble gratitude for its abilities, you're heading in the right direction. Think great thoughts about that amazing body, dream of what it can do and thank it for all it has given.

It may seem slightly odd to talk to yourself in the mirror each day but, hey, if it helps, WHY NOT? Try giving yourself a pep-talk every day to boost your confidence and to make you stop and realise how bloody brilliant you are. My mum once gave me an affirmation necklace that said 'YOU'RE AWESOME' on it. Not 'awesome' in a 1990s surf way, but in a grateful, awe-inspiring way. At first I cringed when I looked at the words and applied them to me, but once I got my head around the meaning, I realised how powerful these sorts of phrases can be.

If we constantly tell ourselves that we are useless at something, we will of course end up being awful at it. If we give ourselves a little pep-talk or have a phrase we say aloud to ourselves each morning, think of the possibilities. If I have a big job ahead that I'm nervous about, I will often come up with a little mantra that I will repeat in my head before going ahead with what is needed. It could be: 'I am strong and capable and will spread happiness with my words', or as simple as 'loving kindness', so that I remember to be kind to myself. I think planting these thoughts in your subconscious really makes a difference to our actions.

Dear **Body**,

Firstly, I would like to say **sorry**. Sorry that I haven't always had the love and respect for you that you so massively deserve. I used to take you for granted and give you little thought and for that I can only apologise.

My mind used to trick me into believing that you were **invincible**. I thought I could dash about on little sleep, erratic fuel and talk badly about you and that you wouldn't mind. I assumed you would tick along just fine and ignore my criticisms. I used to think you weren't good enough as you didn't match up to the images I saw in **magazines**. You were changing and maturing but I still mentally felt like a teenager so I felt trapped in you and uncomfortable. I didn't know how to dress you or move naturally with you and often felt like running from you at a great speed. I took for granted the **energy** you allowed me to use and the places you got me to.

I'm very sorry I occasionally smoked in my twenties. What a horrid and disrespectful way to treat you. I'm sorry there were times when I drank too much and ate too little. I knew deep down that wasn't working for you as you showed me regular signs that you needed more **balance**. I'm sorry I still occasionally stare at you in the mirror and talk disrespectfully to you. Sometimes I just forget the **good** stuff.

Now on to the huge and much needed **THANK YOUs**.

Thank you for growing two beautiful babies. I still don't quite understand how you did it without me having to use my mind in any way at all. Thank you for stretching and expanding and changing my perspective on what you're **capable** of. I could have done without the severe morning sickness bit but, hey, we all have our faults. I guess that was your own way of making me slow down to a different and necessary pace.

Thank you for working **together** with my babies to get them out. Again, my head can't fathom how you did this, but it remains the biggest **game-changing** moment for our relationship. I was and still am in awe of you. You now have slightly saggier skin in areas and fine ghostly white marks to remind me of your ability to stretch and change when needed. I can now even look at those so-called imperfections and feel lucky and proud.

Thank you so much for getting me up Mount Kilimanjaro in my twenties. Such a great **adventure** that I know was difficult and testing for you but in equal measures euphoric. You kept moving and striving and didn't give up even when hit with altitude sickness. Thanks for all those nights on the dance floor where you swung about without care or concern as blood pumped and music worked its way into your every cell. SO much fun!

Thanks for taking that **delicious** food I enjoy so much and converting it into energy so I can get all of the ideas out of my head and make them a reality. Thank you for withstanding heartache, sorrow, over-excitement and for **overcoming** illness and exhaustion. You are a very clever machine that I now love and **respect** so much more. Thank you, dear body. I accept you with all your quirks and characteristics and **vow** to do so for as long as I can.

Thanks,
Fearne

We all abuse and neglect our bodies at some point in ours lives and all make conscious efforts to be kind to it at others. Here is your chance to reflect on what your body has been through in life so far and show thanks and respect to it. Write your own 'Dear Body' letter on the next page . . .

Dear Body,

BODY LANGUAGE

Stance can be applied in the same way. When I was about to have my daughter, Honey, a relative of mine, Jane Cotton, told me that she had watched a gorilla giving birth on film and noticed that the female primate stood with her chest arched to the sky, arms held out wide and head thrown back as she powerfully birthed her offspring. When Jane went into labour herself, she mimicked this movement and had an amazing experience with a huge lack of fear and a lot of power behind it all. I took this on board and tried it out in my own labour. I visualised that incredible gorilla and allowed my body to stretch up and outward to take up space and feel empowered.

If we walk into a room and inside we are feeling quite vulnerable and nervous our body language often seems small and inward. If we trick our minds by letting our bodies tell a different story, others pick up on these signals and will be drawn to our perceived confidence and presence in the room. Maybe when you were younger you managed to blag your way into a club by physically holding yourself in a confident and empowering way? It is a powerful tool that you can use, and eventually your mindset will catch up with your body and be on-board with this new-found confidence.

MOVEMENT

Being active makes me feel alive. It can shift mental struggles while simultaneously charging my body with strength and energy. I'm sure many of you work in an office where you feel numb from sitting at your desk all day. You might be full-time parents with no time to stop and think about your own needs. Some of you might feel you're coping just fine without any exercise in your daily lives, but I really believe that a bit of movement doesn't have to cost an arm and a leg and there are clever ways to fit it around what you do daily.

WALKING'S CHEAP

Sometimes, when I'm cooking for the kids, I'll put some fun music on and we'll all dance about, just to get our bodies on the move. I also love nothing more than just going for a walk come rain or shine. Walking. The simplest of movements that gets overlooked for expensive gym memberships and unflattering Lycra leggings.

I'm having a huge love affair with walking and find it an amazing remedy for many hurdles in life. Walking in the rain, sunshine, gales; in the city, in the park, on my own or with loved ones . . . it is bliss. Rex is at an age where he will walk a short distance before getting tired out so I'll let him switch from walking alongside me to the ride-on board on the back of of Honey's buggy. We will go on adventures looking for worms and slugs and get out of the house to get those legs going.

Walking is the easiest and cheapest form of exercise that gets your heart rate up and lungs expanding. Remembering that the aim is to feel good and get your mind full of positivity which is a much stronger incentive than expecting to look like Gisele by the end of the year. As soon as we give ourselves visual goals of what we want out of exercise, we start to feel let down if things don't go our way. I just want the feel-good bit out of it and always have that in mind if I'm feeling sluggish and low on energy. Moving our bodies will always benefit our minds.

You can make it a part of your day no matter how busy you are. Walking to work rather than driving, taking a walk at lunchtime, walking with your kids, walking after dinner to get some fresh air. It can be done literally anywhere and at any time.

I could walk for hours and at times have. I've done a few treks now that have proved to be some of the best experiences of my life. There's a clarity that sweeps in during these lengthy walks. You're geographically travelling, and therefore your mind moves with you,

shifting perspective and gathering new thoughts.

Me and my dear friend Kye have always hit the pavements when we feel troubled. We've walked for hours through parks, high streets, and fields all with much to say and much willingness to listen. We'll walk and talk until we have no words left and blisters on our heels. So much ground can be covered physically and mentally when you're on the move, so much more than if you're static in a café nattering away in hushed tones.

When I had Honey, a friend who'd recently had a baby would meet me at our local park each week and we'd go for a long, slow hour-long walk and chat about life. We were getting our postnatal bodies moving to help with that healing process and were able to have a much-needed natter, too. Why not arrange to meet up for a weekly walk with a friend to walk and talk together?

I also love to go walking on my own to get ideas. My brain is able to become clear in a much shorter time span when I'm out walking. I don't get distracted by my creature comforts at home or tasks that need doing, I can simply focus on my steps and my breath, leaving my head open to new ideas.

To me, walking is a total joy that gives me something new each time. Ditch the heels, grab a mate and hit the pavement.

WHAT DOES IT FOR ME: YOGA

I have tried most physical workouts over the years. I've climbed a big mountain, I've extensively cycled, run the odd half marathon and danced until my toes bled at dance school. I have taken so much from all of these wonderful and exciting physical adventures but these days what works for me exercise-wise is the odd run and yoga.

I know lots of people can feel a bit apprehensive about yoga, but it's honestly the one activity that navigates me to that blissful territory where my mind and body work in tandem and can be both calm and grow stronger simultaneously. Sometimes in a busy week that one hour of yoga can be the only time I feel truly sane and balanced in this crazy world we live in. Its slow and considered flow allows my body to reach its own potential without striving for a goal or adrenalin rush. It allows my muscles to strengthen without stress and creates a flexibility that raises my energy levels and opens my heart. The cogs stop churning in my overactive mind and a silent bliss blankets the usual noise.

Since taking up yoga I feel physically the best I have ever felt. After Rex was born, my energy levels hit rock bottom and I felt weak from being heavy and pregnant for what felt like forever. My muscles had repositioned themselves in alien territory and new skin folded around my sore bones that hadn't been there before. The thought of the gym felt overwhelming and even imagining a pair of sporty Lycra leggings made my toes curl.

My first yoga class felt strange. I was nervous, and felt like it was the first day of school when I headed to my first lesson. Each position was new and unnatural to my postnatal form and I sweated just moving into a downward dog pose. At first, the physical side of it was all-consuming, so my thoughts naturally drifted to a back pocket of my brain while I concentrated on not falling over or farting.

After about six months I started to understand how my body should feel in each posture, and I found I could go that little bit further with each move. I could explore my own potential and sit on the edge of those boundaries comfortably, but with effort applied. My mind started to open to the undercurrent of spirituality which cements the yogic foundations and I had that lightbulb moment: yoga classes are challenging but not stressful. They're restorative with great results and work perfectly in unison with the mind.

As you can tell, I have a deep love of yoga and all it brings. As soon as I hit that mat it all unravels. If I've had a good day, my head will clear quickly to a new-found clarity, and if I've had a bad day the fog will start to lift gradually and I feel I can breathe properly again.

I go to a local yoga class when I can fit it around the children and work, but mostly I do some simple moves at home in my kitchen. This is the joy of yoga. It goes where you go.

Time can be tight in this day and age, so I've enlisted the help of my dear friend and yoga queen Zephyr Wildman to come up with a restorative sequence that you can do before bed, in your lunch break, or while the baby is napping. It will only take a short amount of time, but will enhance the other twenty-three and a half-odd hours of your day.

A YOGA CLASS FROM ZEPHYR

I went along to a local yoga centre with a mate from Radio 1 about five-and a-half years ago to see what all the fuss was about. The first class I stepped into was led by the incredible Zephyr. I was instantly struck by her calm and grounded words that flowed alongside the movement. She had recently lost her husband to cancer, and was looking after her two young daughters while still teaching her yoga classes. She talked openly to us about her tough time and how yoga was her daily grounding during this period of grieving. Her strength and attitude drew me in instantly.

After this serendipitous moment I became a Vinyasa yoga devotee, and loved getting to Zephyr's classes whenever I could. Over the years we have become close friends and I love our friendship very much.

Zephyr has kindly made this calming sequence – which would be perfect before bedtime – that I hope you'll enjoy greatly. The breaths should move with the poses, so each move signals an inhale or exhale. You can, of course, hold the poses if you want a really good stretch, or to slow right down mentally, but if you prefer a bit of flow then move through these moves with grace and ease and with deep, long breaths that complete each pose.

Remember to make each movement count. Make sure energy is rushing through to your toes and fingertips as you stretch up and out as much as you can. Keep your muscles active and strong throughout to help with strength and balance. Work at a pace that feels good to you. Keep your mind focused on the breath and its importance, and this will help to clear your mind.

1) Start off with your legs crossed. Breathe in as you stretch your arms out in front of you, so that your forehead travels towards the floor, feeling your hips open and your spine lengthening. Hold here. Still with your arms out-stretched, gently take your arms across the floor to the right of you, bending at the hips. Hold and then repeat this to the left hand side.

2) Slowly return to your cross legged seated posture. Place your right hand on the floor at a right angle to your body, bending your elbow.

Then reach your left hand up above your head and over to the right side, creating a straight line from your fingertips down to your hip. Hold the pose, and then repeat on the other side.

3) Bring your arms back down. Place your left hand on your right knee and gently twist at the hips so that your right arm travels behind you and your finger tips or hand presses against the floor, ensuring that your back remains straight. Breathe in to feel the length-ening of your spine and hold. Exhale and then repeat to the other side. This is a wonderful twist!

4) Come back to seated posture. Extend your arms in front of you, with your left arm slightly below your right. Then bend both your elbows and wrap your right forearm over your left. Press your palms together if you can. With your arms in this position, bend at the base of the spine so that you're looking up. Then slowly curve your spine the other way so that you are looking down. Repeat with your left forearm on top. Release your arms and come back to your crosslegged posture. Place your hands flat on the floor behind you. Arch your back and feel the stretch of your spine.

5) Now come to all fours. Arch your back, push your belly down and your bum up. Power energy through your arms and look to the sky.

6) Then tuck your bum in, arch your back up and continue to keep your arms energised and strong, with your head tucked under.

7) Come back to all fours. Extend your right leg behind you so your toes are flexed and pushing into the floor, keeping your leg strong and straight. Place your right palm flat on the ground in line with your left toes. Your left knee should be directly over your left foot. Take your left arm straight up, turning your torso slightly to the left for a nice stretch.

8) Bring your left hand back to your knee, then take your forearm down onto the ground, and bring your right forearm down to join it. Keep your right leg strong and straight behind you and make sure your left knee is still directly over your left foot.

9) Now take your weight onto your right knee so that your left leg can straighten and stretch out in front of you.

Outstretch your arms so that your hands are either side of your foot to assist with this stretch. Repeat moves 7–9 with the other leg.

10) Come to all fours then stretch up with straight arms and legs so that your bum is in the air and your palms are flat on the floor with your fingers splayed. Imagine a straight line from your hands to your bum, and your bum down to your feet. Don't worry if your heels aren't fully flat on the floor.

11) Float your left leg upwards and bend at the knee. Hold the pose, ensuring that

your breath continues to flow and your shoulders remain square to the floor.

12) Float your leg that is in the air through your arms so that it is now bent and flat on the floor in front of you. Extend your right leg out straight behind you. Keep your palms on the floor firmly in front of you to ensure your back remains straight. Make sure your sit bones are planted firmly on the floor. Then stretch both hands out to the right of you, with your head down, to feel a nice stretch along the left of your body.

13) Bring your right leg forward and lean over it,

holding the pose. Then place your right hand on your left knee and turn at the base of the spine so your left hand travels behind you. Come back to position 10 and repeat steps 11-13 with the other leg.

14) Now come to a sitting posture where both legs are outstretched, your hands are on the floor at your sides and your chest is lifted whilst you hold your belly firmly in. Imagine a piece of string pulling the crown of your head towards the sky. Hold the pose and breathe deeply.

15) Come down to lying position with your back on the ground and your arms either side of you. Bend your knees and tuck your feet close to your bum.

16) Take your arms above your head and use your feet to push your hips as high into the air as possible. Hold the pose breathing into all those areas that feel tight. Release.

17) Now bend your knees and take your legs to the left of you, with your right arm stretched out the other way and your face turned to that direction. Hold the pose, then turn the other way.

18) Bring your legs back to the centre and turn your knees outward with your feet pressed together, and your hands resting on your lower abdomen. Breathe in and out deeply and recognise how the whole of your body feels.

BREATHING

To round off this chapter I'm going to hit on BREATHING! This is a huge part of yoga, and a huge tool in your arsenal. How simple is breathing? Well, not very, it seems. I realised through yoga that as soon as I feel unnerved or anxious, I hold my breath at the top of its inhale. My chest puffs out and solidifies with a spiky fear until I'm forced to quickly pant and exhale. I hate this feeling. Yoga is helping me to keep a steady fluid breath that will help my mind and physically get things working as they should inside.

Breath is so powerful. It can calm our physical and mental state very quickly indeed. 'Take a deep breath'... how many times have we had that advice forced down our throats at a seemingly inappropriate tense moment? But it does work. Long, deep and steady breaths level out our nervous systems and calm our every cell while pulling the mind back to a gentle wave of consciousness. This is my happy place!!! And I hope it can be yours, too.

Summary

**HAPPY BODY =
HAPPY MIND.**

Look after your body and it will work beautifully together with your mind.

**BE NICE TO
YOURSELF.**

Thank your body and see the good in it, every day.

**GET
MOVING.**

However small or simple the activity, get moving and let the endorphins flow.

WHAT DOES HAPPY BODY LOOK LIKE TO YOU?

Write one word or draw a picture here that sums it up

HAPPY *Families*

Family: a clan, a gang, a related community. A deep-rooted love that always brings me back home. It makes me instantly remember what I truly care about, and the morals I base my life upon. Those family foundations in life where blood or deep love connects us can be so very powerful and beautiful.

I love that feeling of belonging in my family. Whether it be my direct family who are my world, my extended family who I can fall comfortably in line with, or 'friend' families who offer comfort and familiarity, they're the people that connect the dots between your past, present and future.

MAKE THE MOST OF FAMILY

I didn't give family life much thought growing up. What's going on around you as a kid is your 'normal' and you expect everyone else is having similar experiences elsewhere.

It's only when I became a parent myself that I truly understood family life and recognised its importance. Others may have made this discovery much earlier in life, and without having children of their own, but for me it was a breakthrough moment. I had taken for granted many aspects of the family set-up before this epiphany and also hadn't realised that the dynamic of a family is constantly shifting, so is therefore a very delicate structure: babies are being born, older relatives are passing on, children are growing up and forming their own ideas, some family members may move away or get lost in a tangle of disagreement. The relationships and bonds in a family are forever evolving, morphing to fit around life's natural progression.

Growing up, I was lucky enough to have two strong, yet very different, parental figures that guided me through my childhood and my teenage years. My mum is a very tenacious female figure in my life who has bold ideas and puts a lot of force behind them. She has always given me that extra boost of determination when needed. My dad is the calm anchor to the family, always offering unbiased and grounded advice when asked. I'm forever grateful for

the support and freedom they gave me as I was growing up and working so young.

When I was growing up, my family was of an average size, with a gang of cousins who we holidayed with and four grandparents that lived until I was in my twenties. I am lucky enough to be able to take myself back down memory lane to scenes of us all camping in the summer and gorging on fresh baguettes. Growing up in the 1980s in a working-class suburb of London, with this gang around me, felt pretty good. We would gather at Christmas, birthdays and for summer barbecues and enjoy the simple pleasures of laughter and food.

Now that I'm older and find myself in my own new tribe, I am getting to grips with the detailed inner workings of our gang and how we can be at our strongest for each other. I feel fortunate that my husband and I have a strong union and friendship that allows us to work together and share the same vision for how we want to raise our children.

There is an inexplicable strength that lies within a family, and that can be an incredibly powerful force. Barriers are broken down quickly, and courageous and selfless acts take place in a heartbeat. I've experienced this first-hand from many lovely people in my family when times have been tough. Being on the receiving end of these selfless, loving gestures has been unexpected and game-changing for me. When I had a terribly black time a while ago, before I had seen a doctor or even considered it might be depression, my aunty and mum came over to my house with veggie sausage rolls and coffee, for a gentle, kind chat. Their advice and words, and simple offering of food, helped to steer me in the right direction to seek help. I didn't feel judged or pressured because a true, deep-rooted love was being given to me with open arms. Family love at its best.

Another surprising moment was at my nan's funeral. She was our last grandparent to leave planet Earth and we all felt rather anxious and tearful about the funeral. The ceremony itself was emotional and heavy, but as soon as we all congregated at the local pub for a drink and reminisced, the love in that room sent us all into fits of laughter as we recalled funny stories and acknowledged that common theme that linked us all to the core. We reconnected with my nan's ninety-two-year-old brother Haydn too. He is my connection to Nan and carries that family resemblance, thought process and history that I sometimes forget to give thanks for.

When you feel lost in life, or like something is missing, try and give thanks for those close to you. They seem so permanent and obvious in their position in your life that they can get overlooked at times. I'm part of a gang and, whether it all runs smoothly or not, I'm privileged to have people around me that can see past any quarrel and will forever hold me in their hearts.

HELLO TO . . . HAYDN

As I get older I feel much more in tune with what makes me happy, and much more courageous in sourcing that inner well of goodness. I can let go of the past that bit easier and not feel too scared for the future, either.

When my dear nan, Ruby, passed away, I felt a deep, nostalgic sadness. At her funeral I reconnected with her brother Haydn who was the life and soul of the occasion. Even though he had just lost his only sibling, he managed to keep up the morale by telling wonderful stories and making us all laugh. Walking away I felt so inspired, and realised that a greater sense of perspective must be reached as years pass us by. I email Haydn most weeks now and love hearing his views on life. Here follows his own thoughts on happiness after an almighty and glorious ninety-two years on Earth. What an insight. Thank you, Uncle Haydn.

HAYDN: Have I cracked happiness? I am sure I was never an unhappy person. I lived for people to laugh with me, and always tried to find the amusing side of life. I never sold doom and gloom – it was never part of my ethos. When faced with adversity, I've alway managed to stay positive. I always try to think 'what's the point of being miserable?' Only by looking on the bright side will things improve.

My first memory of feeling happy was when I was four and a half. It was Christmas, 1928. That time of year was joyful, despite the fact that money was very scarce: it meant paper chains which we stuck together and used to decorate the rooms downstairs – all great fun for my sister Ruby and me. Perhaps my first memory of snow was at that time, and it fell thick and heavy. The following year, I was allowed to roll about in it despite the discomfort that followed – the wet overcoat and much more. It was a wonderful experience and remained in my memory as a very happy occasion. Really, it was a selfish act and caused extra work for my loving mother who had to dry me out, but I thoroughly enjoyed the experience.

I was never more at ease than when I was with others, regardless of who they were: family, friends or strangers. Sadly, I lacked a formal education, but I learned to be interested in what people had to say – listen carefully, you will learn something every time. I also learned never to speak over other folk talking to me.

Presently, happiness is being able to look after Pamela, the mother of our children, who has no memory of yesterday and only spasmodic glimpses of our past life together. We overcome this by looking at photos – fortunately I always took masses of pictures, and I am blessed with patience, which helps no end. My other passion, which gives me much happiness, is my commitment to leaving a legacy to our children which will help them and, in turn, support our grandchildren in higher education and assist them onto the first rung of the property ladder. We are so fortunate to have loving children.

In my younger days my 'happiness modes' came from enjoyment just for me, a self-centred attitude which I overcame after one of my advisers at work told me, 'Whatever you do, just be sure you give the credit for your achievements to your staff'. I found that gave me more pleasure and happiness than anything I had experienced before.

Do these happy moments stand out? Absolutely! I never look back at unhappiness. Learn a lesson from it, by all means, but don't dwell on it. It serves no useful purpose.

'UNCONVENTIONAL' FAMILIES

However small, big, loud, shy, retiring, or ever-growing your family is, they're yours and you are part of it. The shape and size of your family doesn't matter, it's the feeling of belonging which does.

Our set-up has never been conventional but it works for us and feels fun and bustling, which is how we like it. When I met my husband he already had two children. Being a stepmother is an honour and something I take great care in trying to get right. I'm not trying to be their mum as they have that role model in their life already. I'm around to give support, love and stability when they need it and to have a clear and honest relationship with them. My husband and I have been very open with my stepchildren from the moment we met – I think communication is key to making everyone feel safe and comfortable. If all involved understand what is going on around them, and what changes may take place, then you can all go on a journey together that isn't scary or a shock.

When we got pregnant with our first child, Rex, we told my stepchildren, Arthur and Lola, before anyone else. They then became a vital part of that pregnancy and life experience. They eagerly helped welcome Rex into our family home and became

Families are such a wonderful mixture of joy, safety and irritation! Each family member will offer you something whether it be from a positive or negative place.

Without too much thought, quickly write down the first word that springs to mind when you think of each family member. After you've written this list go back and work out what can be gained from embracing each of these words and what they offer you in life, whether that's support or a learning.

MUM: GRANDAD:

DAD: GRANDMA:

STEPMUM: GRANDAD:

STEPDAD: AUNTY:

BROTHER: AUNTY:

SISTER: UNCLE:

BROTHER: UNCLE:

SISTER: COUSIN:

BROTHER: COUSIN:

SISTER: COUSIN:

GRANDMA: COUSIN:

doting older siblings, excited by their new team member. When we decided to get married, again the kids were the first to know. They helped pick our wedding cake flavours and music for the big day and had a role that felt exciting and uniting. Our second child, Honey, is now the youngest member of our family unit and, again, the older siblings are so helpful and adorable with her as they knew what was going on every step of the way.

Blended families are much more prevalent in recent years, but there's still a newness and uncertainty around how it should all work. We don't give it much thought these days as this just IS our family set-up. We know no different and we have made it work for us.

PARENTS AND CHILDREN

Being a parent can be particularly overwhelming, but I wouldn't change it for the world. I can't speak for dads, but being a mum is EVERYTHING: it's extreme joy, extreme exhaustion, extreme frustration, extreme elation, extreme pride, extreme worry and everything else in between.

I never take being a mum for granted but I do find some aspects of parenting tricky, as it's so overwhelming seeing these

Draw a family portrait or stick in your favourite family photo here.

two creatures I grew in my belly navigate their way through this weird old life, with me as one of their main guides.

I've been broody since I can remember, but motherhood certainly turned out to be very different to how I had imagined. The love I feel is a love I couldn't have envisaged before giving birth. I love my husband to the soul but it's a different kind of love with my children. No more or less, just different. This love feels so huge at times that it gets wound up in frustration or worry and makes me doubt if I'm doing a good enough job. This love makes me care so much that I, like many other mothers, feel I'm not doing my best. This part of motherhood I did not expect. I thought I'd feel carefree and laid back, but that is very rarely the case. This is a realisation that happens overnight. One minute you're pregnant and full of anticipation and excitement, the next you've had the baby and are heaped with worry and self-doubt. Luckily, these new and unfamiliar feelings are compacted with a pure love so strong that the worrying wafts in and out of the scene.

I clearly remember how I felt when we first took Rex home, and how I couldn't quite believe that there would be no midwife to give me round-the-clock advice. How on earth would I keep this small human alive and still manage to clean my own teeth and take the odd shower? That first step into the unknown territory of parenting felt strange but time helps you settle into your groove of having a family. I'm at a stage now where we all know our role within our close family unit, and have a clear idea of what will and won't work. We have plenty of blissful times seeped in laughter and family joy, and while there are moments of chaos, I know that underneath the pile of dishes in the sink, and beneath that peanut butter-smeared Lego on the floor, is a thick layer of that family love that I am so blessed to have.

I still get overwhelmed with the love I feel for my kids and the love they give me. I feel like the luckiest person on earth when I look at their faces. I love being a mum and having this magical dynamic with my kids and stepkids. It has brought so much energy and soul to my life and for that I am full of the deepest thanks.

For those whose life agenda doesn't include becoming a parent, that same love is, of course, still there for the taking from the people around you, whether that's parents and siblings, or nieces and nephews. Stop and take note of it; feel the layer of love underneath all the mayhem and let yourself feel full on it.

Seeing things from another angle sometimes helps us walk down that road to happiness. See if this approach can help you with any family tensions you currently have – and if you have some pencils handy, why not colour the family tree here in?!

MUM GUILT

Running a family and being a working woman throws up many new challenges that I hadn't even imagined.

I grew up in a working-class family, and lived a comfortable life due to my parents' constant hard work and organisational skills. I paid little attention to this as it was our 'normal' and I was too busy being a kid. Mum worked up to three jobs at a time, as an orthodontist nurse, cleaner, and clothing company delivery driver, while my dad was, and still is, a busy sign writer. This work ethic rubbed off on me in a huge way, and is at the root of how I run my life.

I want to work, and I love my job very much, so have to find a balance that works for me and my children and stepchildren. This causes me much grief as I'm never sure I'm doing my best at any of it. I often wish there were at least four more hours in the day where I could do all the stuff I have on my ever-growing checklist. Mum guilt is an element of parenthood that I'm still working on. I find talking to other working mums really helps, as they can offer up great advice and their own personal stories. There will always be pros and cons to working, or choosing not to. Knowing you've made a decision for the right reason, for YOU, should really be enough, but I have to constantly remind myself of this.

I feel very fortunate that after all these years of working I now work partly from home and can choose to put my full attentive energy into projects I really adore. I feel very lucky to have got to this point in my career, and hope that by going to work and thoroughly enjoying it, I'm demonstrating to my kids that it is possible, and that they can work hard and achieve their desired goals. You have to grasp the positives from your own situation and remember how that choice will affect your kids in a positive way, whether you're out working or not.

TRICKY FAMILIES

The network of family outside of our little home units will always be expanding and complex, and it's almost a dead certainty that you'll not see eye-to-eye with certain members of your extended family at some point.

I was aware of struggles and tensions in parts of my family when I was growing up, but understood little about them. There were some family members that wouldn't speak to others, and hushed tones in certain situations. But I don't think this is unusual in any family tribe – families are made up of very different minds and spirits who, after all, just happen to be blood-related.

I have had complicated relationships with some members of

my family that I regularly mull over and get anxious about, and I'm not sure that side of it is ever easy. But, like with anything, it offers something to learn from. These tribes we've created or have fallen into are a constant reminder of what we personally need to work on or develop. Families are complicated, but I think if we all get to know what our own roles are within them, then we can start to unravel behavioural patterns and be slightly more aware of the needs of those around us. What do you feel your role is in your own family unit? Are you the organiser? The troublemaker? The boundary pusher? The mediator? The listener? Do you feel comfortable in that role, or do you feel pressured into it by others? If you feel like you're carrying more weight than you should, or are in a role you don't want any more, is there potential for this to change? Is there a way you could delegate what feels like too much for you? Or, maybe, do you see those around you struggling? Is there a way you can help unburden them? Only you will know these delicate situations and how much change is possible.

It might sound slightly grating, but the people that cause us to constantly react are usually the ones who are teaching us the most. They're the ones making us dig deeper and take a look at our own actions and feelings around family life. It's how we deal with those situations that counts. I love my family and extended family very much, so to be totally honest, I don't feel comfortable writing about

Who is the person you are concerned about seeing at your next family gathering?

. . . .

What do they do that causes you to react in a negative way?

. . . .

How does it make you feel?

. . . .

How do you react to this behavioural pattern?

. . . .

How would you like the next family gathering to play out?

. . . .

How you would like to react if tension arises?

. . . .

How would it feel to say goodbye to the old patterns and stories you've experienced? Be as honest as you can, as sometimes it's a tough tie to let go of.

. . . .

I mentally go through this checklist when I know I'm facing a similar situation, and it helps me clear my mind of expectations. Freedom! You're in control. Get visualising.

the intricacies of our own inner workings and dynamics. But what I will say is this: in any family there are easy relationships and ones which require more work. We all face these challenges in life. I've been part of and witness to family feuds and tension on occasions and have reacted differently and from different perspectives. I always strive to react from a place of love and with an open heart but I do get dragged into the drama and the past. I know over the years I've lashed out and hurled loaded words out of frustration and resentment, rather than looking at the bigger picture and keeping my heart and mind open. All we can do is strive to unburden ourselves of anger and frustration and embrace a more positive perspective. It can only lead to more peace and, ultimately, happiness.

VISUALISE THE GOOD

If you know a family get-together is looming and there could be rumblings of tension or an ongoing negative situation, why not try and run though a positive scenario in your head en route? Firstly, try to let go of your preconceptions. If we assume certain scenarios will take place and particular words will be spoken, then we are already setting ourselves up for a fall. We have pre-conceived ideas of what's going to happen, so they'll more than likely be met with what we are expecting. Instead, why not try to do the exact opposite? Travel there with an open mind, knowing that there may be uncomfortable moments, but that you'll be okay and that you are in control of your reactions. Whatever you are met with, you can then digest and react to it in a controlled way. Remember that no one has power over you, even if it feels like it. This is easier said than done but, like most things in life, with a little practise it gets much easier. Think of it as an experiment for the day. Think to yourself: 'What would happen if I reacted in a totally different way to the way I normally do?'

Perhaps your aunty always brings up something embarrassing from your past and you react with anger and passive aggressive tones, before leaving abruptly for a journey home loaded with rage-fuelled rants. What if, when these moments occur, you take her to one side and in a loving way explain to her how uncomfortable this makes you feel and that you are hoping for a family get-together filled with laughter and love. This may be a completely unnatural thing to do, but it might just break the chain of behaviour that's been continuing for years.

Maybe your sister always acts like a baby when she is with your parents, which in turn makes them dote on her in a way they don't you. Your usual instinct and reaction might be to close down and shut off your own communication with them. You create a ripple effect that sends them deeper into this dynamic, and you feel alienated and annoyed. You could instead try to view where your sister is at in life before you react. Perhaps she needs more attention and love from others than you do. This is her own personal weakness and it doesn't have to affect you and your own happiness. You could either openly ask your sister why her behaviour changes in these moments, as she may not have even noticed it herself, or you could just let it play out each time you're all together, but step back and not let it affect how you interact with them.

If you do have family turmoil, then why not use your journey to these gatherings to visualise it all going exactly as you wish? Imagine a reality you want. Think of it as a fun experiment. It might not work right away, but it will alter your mindset enough to embrace whatever lies ahead.

Sometimes we can all be guilty of enjoying the drama. It gives us topics to talk about on the way home, allows us to release some inner rage, or simply feels natural, as it has become a pattern in your life. If you are happy jogging along like this then do what feels right, but if you really want change and are tired of any repetitive hurt and angst, then start visualising what you want to see in front of you and make it happen.

GIVE THANKS

The most important thing to remember is that there will always be tough moments within family life, but they are not exclusive to my family or your family – we all experience them sometimes. I think as long as everyone communicates honestly and approaches situations of potential conflict from a place of love, peace can be found. Don't be afraid to break habits of the past; don't accept awkwardness or tension because it has always been there. Try to solve it, and if you can't – learn from it.

Above all, give thanks to the gang you're in. Whether this be blood family or a tribe you've chosen to be part of, give thanks to the ones that make you laugh, the ones that challenge you the most, and to the power that your combined love can offer. Know that no matter what is going on in your clan, LOVE cements the foundations. Each member of your family was born from love and has it pumping through their veins, whether they show it or not. Lean in to that love, encourage that love and give it right back.

Summary

MAKE THE MOST OF FAMILY.

Take time to remember the things they have done for you and acknowledge the happiness their support can bring.

STEER AWAY FROM 'MUM GUILT'.

There's no right or wrong so don't beat yourself up. Whether you need or choose to work, or you're a stay-at-home mum, your kids will gain from your ethics and love no matter what.

VISUALISE THE GOOD.

Don't assume family drama before it happens; approach it with an open heart and mind.

WHAT DOES HAPPY **FAMILIES**
LOOK LIKE TO YOU?

Write one word or draw a picture here that sums it up

HAPPY *Thanks*

Saying thank you is such an easily exercised gesture that, sometimes, we forget its meaning. We say it when someone makes us a cup of tea. We breathe it when the sun shines. We growl it when really we mean the opposite. We snarl it sarcastically to get a response. We shout it aloud to the skies when a long-awaited moment arrives. We hear it all day long spoken in these different contexts but not often understanding its sometimes throwaway facade. But when those words are spoken and meant sincerely, tectonic plates in your own world move and your horizon expands.

A HABIT TO LEARN

Learning to live with gratitude is a habit and one worth practising. I guess it's like remembering to drink lots of water in the day so you feel hydrated and energised. It doesn't always naturally slip into your life, but once it's part of your day, you don't have to think about it so much.

Saying 'thank you' is a habit we weave into our everyday lives from a young age. We were all taught it to sound polite in conversation, but it's as adults that we can really unearth the power of those words and feelings. Feeling gratitude – real, whole gratitude – comes in spontaneous waves when you're on the edge of sheer bliss, where it feels only right to smile and beam a big THANK YOU for the simple things that lie in front of you. Saying it and really meaning it can massively awaken your senses and perspective to what there is in life to feel thanks for.

I love to say thanks in many ways. Letters, cards, flowers, hugs, kisses. I've been brought up to say thank you in the most obvious way you can, with meaning backing it up. I squirm at the thought of forgetting to use its full force appropriately, and hope that those who have helped me in any way over the years know how much I deeply appreciate it. I've always been bad at asking for help or for favours, so when someone does something genuinely lovely off their own back, I'm blown away. I instantly remember how gorgeous humans can be and the power of that interaction. Equally, when others show their thanks, it's heart-pumpingly divine. You know that you've aided that person in some way and that it meant something to them. This could be intentional or unintentional, but it will still feel dreamy.

FEELING LUCKY

 When we are feeling blue, or even worse, black, our main focus is on what we feel is lacking in our lives. We lose sight of the precious and dear things right in front of us, and have pin-sharp focus on what we DON'T have. Practising gratitude enables you to look through a magnifying glass at the things you know you feel lucky and happy to have, pulling out of focus the 'lacking' and 'want' and boosting the comfort and contentment you have in your current life.

The wheels of our economy are spun by the feeling that we don't quite have enough. That one super-shiny pair of life-changing loafers might just be the thing that makes you feel complete. That new turbo-charged, sexy sports car might just fill the void you're feeling. That new marshmallow-cosy couch could just set your front room off perfectly and make you feel more in control

Today's date: ....

What I'm grateful for:

....

Today's date: ....

What I'm grateful for:

....

Today's date: ....

What I'm grateful for:

....

Today's date: ....

What I'm grateful for:

....

Today's date: ....

What I'm grateful for:

....

Today's date: ....

What I'm grateful for:

....

of life. Not everyone is caught up in this constant cycle of want, but most of us are on some level. I have been witness to quite a few people who are completely trapped in its grasp. Some of them unknowingly and some very openly. One dear friend is very honest about their complete love of splurging on clothes and furniture and they do get joy from it – as we all do when we buy or attain something we are passionate about – but it's never going to provide the wholesome, long-term contentment, that we all seek from within.

At times, buying into the fantasy of having stuff and needing stuff helps us avoid looking at what is really going on in our lives on a deeper level. Being thankful for what we already have – whether material or otherwise – is always a good starting point.

WHY GRATITUDE IS GREAT

If you feel you haven't achieved enough, you haven't lived enough, you AREN'T enough, then you're only looking at a tiny piece of the puzzle that makes up the intricate and unique person that is you. You're illuminating the lack of certain moments and qualities in your life rather than scoping out the bigger picture. I do this all the time! So let's say hello to our new best mate: GRATITUDE.

Along he comes on his white stallion with his shield in hand. He is here to ward off the self-attack and make you see what is really going on. Probably some pretty good stuff.

Gratitude, when truly meant and practiced, allows us to highlight those basic things we may have overlooked that can be powerful enough to lift you out of a pretty blue place. I try and do this when things get tough. When I hit my big patch of depression, it felt very hard to cling onto anything. I knew I was grateful, and I mean truly grateful, for my family but with that came a feeling of guilt that I wasn't doing my best to be there for them. My gratitude was soaked through with this darkness, so I would turn even that tiny positive into a negative.

Getting out of this pit required a combination of time, energy, people and thought processes, but once I started to climb that rickety ladder I could truly breathe life into that gratitude and magnify what I knew I had. I could peek one eye out of my dark sunglasses and see I had many people around me that loved me: my family and dear and special mates that I could talk to when I felt the time was right.

Then the fact that I could paint or go for a run if I chose to came into focus. I had that freedom, and remembering that brought a lighter shade of blue to the forefront. I could listen to music and let that wash through my muddled head. Noticing that felt good, clear, lighter. Reminiscing about glorious summer holidays spent with dear friends, memories which no one could take away from me. I could take long walks by the river and let my eyes focus on tiny ripples of water and feel the breeze on my cheeks. This was possible, too. There were other options that I could focus on and ultimately give thanks for. True thanks that this was all around me and could be a greater part of my story once my perspective shifted further. Even when you feel you have nothing in life, there will be something near you or something you have experienced that you can push your gratitude towards. It may seem tiny and insignificant but it will be so worth it. It could just be the seed that grows and grows into a mighty tree.

A CLOSE-TO-HOME EXAMPLE

Like many of you, I have encountered some incredible people in my life who, when faced with extreme adversity, have found that spark of something that makes them feel alive and they have grabbed it by the heart and pummelled it with gratitude. They set life and love alight, even when both seemed scarce and desperate, and they started down a new path of thinking towards more positive territory. This sort of mindset and way of life is constantly

With so much negativity in the world it is important for us to show a bit of **positivity**, no matter how small, whenever we can. Write down or draw something that makes you smile here.

Now take a photo of this page and post it on social media! **Happiness shared**!

inspiring to me, and I can only draw on these special individuals' stories to get better at it myself.

I'm particularly lucky that someone very close to me has this exact attitude, and that is the person I'm married to. My husband Jesse lost his mum out of the blue when life seemed to be rocketing along just fine. One minute he had a mum, the next he didn't. This devastating new hole in his life seemed completely unfair and dis-combobulating. His compass spun out wildly as he tried to grab onto anything that could help. A pretty shitty time. They were very close indeed. Krissy had instilled in him beautiful social skills and a lust for adventure and gave him sturdy support when he really needed it. Without her, his world didn't make sense.

He tried the numbing method to some extent, but more recently in life he has taken a step further into it all and got to know how it really felt to be without her. It has been painful and confusing at times, but he is constant in one notion, and that is gratitude. He talks so fondly of her and his memories are loaded with laughter and eye-rolls as he recalls moments of love and hilarity. He is grateful for every moment she spent in his life and has mountains of thanks for her strength and tenacity when he was growing up. He has turned his loss and sorrow into a new story of memories and inspiration by being thankful for her existence at all times. I find this truly inspiring and a firm reminder of how powerful gratitude can be.

THE LITTLE THINGS

We don't just have to be thankful for the momentous occasions, either – the little things deserve a shower of gratitude, too. This is how we can get gratitude in our lives every day. And if we can feel true thanks for the stuff we normally overlook, it can make us much more aware of what's really going on, too. For instance, right now I'm sat in my kitchen on a bar stool typing on my laptop. That could be my one sentence about what is going on for me right now, but if I really use gratitude to work its magic, I can actually start to feel the night-time summer breeze wafting through the nearby window; I can hear the call of crows on the church wall nearby; I can feel thankful for the sweet cup of tea I just drank; and whisper a soft thanks for the peaceful calm floating around my house because my dreamy babies are asleep in their beds. This little non-spectacular moment just switched up to be pretty special. It's taking the focus away from the negatives that could make an appearance in your script, by covering everything else with gratitude.

THE TRICKY
(BUT REWARDING) BIT

Now comes the really tricky part. Being thankful for the bad stuff. I don't deal well with this one so even writing about it is making my hands slightly stiffen and my mouth curl at the thought. Why should we be grateful for the downright unfair and awful? Why should we say thanks to people who have done us wrong and bruised us deeply? Well, you certainly don't have to, but it helps to make that moment, and the fear that surrounds it, even smaller.

For example, I have talked a lot in this book about times when I've felt overcome with sadness and anger and confusion. During those times I wasn't able to see through any of that thick and dirty murk. Even now, to actually feel gratitude for these moments seems impossible, but when I manage to feel just a drop of it, the load feels lighter. So, here goes.

I do know that from these times of darkness have evolved pure light. Would I be writing this book – *Happy* – now if I hadn't experienced the extreme other side of the coin? Probably not. So thanks for that. Would I have the same empathy if I hadn't felt so low myself? Maybe not. So, thank you dark times. Would I have met the great people in my life if I hadn't been so desperately climbing over the hurdles of unhappiness? Most definitely not.

Even moments that feel like tragic mistakes can be thrown some gratitude as they would have taught you at least one new thing about yourself. Maybe those moments have taught you to not judge others so much. Maybe they've shown you how strong you can be when needed. Maybe they've introduced you to a whole new side of life. When you're in the epicentre of these times, nothing seems possible, but when the storm passes, there, among a lot of rubble and ash, will lie a few little moments to be grateful for. Those small acorns might grow into mighty oak trees that you had never even imagined. It won't make those terrible times disappear, but this thanks might just make living with them that bit more bearable.

I still struggle with the concept of showing gratitude for the unwanted bits in life, but it's getting much easier with time and practise.

LITTLE THINGS

If you're stuck for ideas, then getting down with nature is a really good, instant way to throw a bit of thanks around. Nature is a majestic artwork that is constantly changing and surprising us. There is always something new to see and appreciate in nature, even if you're not quite ready to put that focus on your personal life just yet.

Just walk out of your front door and take a stroll for five minutes, take a few deep breaths and look at the sky around you while opening your ears to the nearby sounds. You might hear some birds, see a waft of pink in the evening sky or feel some light rain on your eyelids: all tiny magical wonders to be grateful for.

Start small by making those tiny things really count and work your way up to what is going on inside further down the line. There will be a little magic out there somewhere if you look hard enough.

Every now and again, I write down my gratitude list, as putting pen to paper seems to help me focus even more acutely on the thanks I want to show. This is one really easy way to get gratitude woven into your thinking, so you can use it as a handy tool whenever it's needed. Even if nothing particularly eventful happened in your day, look for the magic that was perhaps going on around you.

Write down a list of things that made you feel alive, or happy for that brief moment. These can be big, wonderful 'thank yous' for the extraordinary or they can be teeny tiny nuggets that felt significant to you.

Being **grateful** is easy if you start small. Give thanks for the teeny-tiny things in life and watch the power of that gratitude build into something great. These tiny **building blocks** give all of us a better perspective on what is going on around us and let us view the positives in tougher times. Write down small things you are grateful for in each box and watch the heart **fill up.**

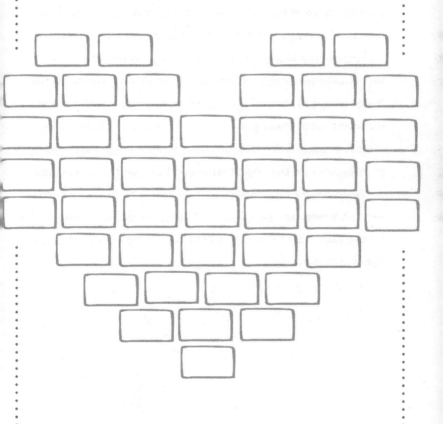

HERE ARE MINE FOR TODAY:

- Thank you for my children's laughter that seems to rattle through every bone in my body, awakening my soul each time.
- Thank you for the sunshine that hit my cheeks when I was in the garden earlier.
- Thanks to the few new people I met at work today, who were charismatic and engaging. Always inspiring.
- I feel hugely grateful for every mouthful of food that went into my system today, giving me energy I didn't think I had.
- Thank you for that big old moon in the sky tonight. Beautiful.
- I feel grateful for the tricky relationships I have with some people in my life as they continue to drive me to take a closer look at myself and how I can react better.
- Thanks for my warm bed I'm about to slip into. The best feeling.
- I feel hugely grateful for all of those I love and those who love me. Such comfort.

Write down your own gratitude list here.

Today I am thankful for:

. . . .

. . . .

. . . .

. . . .

. . . .

. . . .

. . . .

. . . .

. . . .

. . . .

. . . .

How are you feeling today?

HAPPY	SAD	SPARKY
ENERGISED	LOW	OVERWHELMED
EXCITED	BOUNCY	NUMB
JOYFUL	DRENCHED	PRICKLY
FRUITY	HEAVY	STUCK
LOVING	CONFUSED	TIRED
SCARED	BUBBLY	FRAGILE

Summary

USE GRATITUDE.

If you're feeling down, noticing what you're thankful for can help you recognise the good in the world.

SEEK OUT LITTLE THINGS.

Look for small things to appreciate each day, not just momentous occasions.

THANK THE BAD STUFF.

Try to see the lesson, and be thankful for this stuff, too.

WHAT DOES HAPPY **THANKS** LOOK LIKE TO YOU?

Write one word or draw a picture here that sums it up

HAPPY *Shared*

This might just be the most important part of the book. It's about human connection, the magic that happens when people work together, give and share; it's the most powerful exchange of energy, where inexplicable events can take place. From the hug I receive every morning from my three-year-old, Rex, to the happy hellos at my local coffee shop, these are small moments that make being human bloody lovely.

And when those mountains need to be climbed, they can be climbed with the support of great friends. I feel very lucky to have a bevy of mates who I can offload to, and they can do the same with me. Even just picking up the phone to my mate, Lolly, for a quick chat can be enough to change my mindset on a worry or drama. Listening ears, empathetic reasoning and love felt, or honest words; these offer the biggest help there is.

PART OF A PACK

I believe we've all learned to think as independent humans. We strive for what each of us believes we need, and get competitive and single-minded about pursuing our vision. We have forgotten that we are all part of one moving, vibrating energy that ripples across the surface of the earth, an intricate structure of energy that is completely connected. Somewhere down the line, we have let this way of thinking slip, and when this happens we can get trapped in loneliness and isolation and find ourselves at war with others, viewing them as enemies or reasons to feel fear. This doesn't have to be the case. Strangers or people who think completely differently to us can sometimes offer so much to our own lives. New thought processes, a fresh perspective or a new avenue to walk down. Connection is the key to opening your heart and mind, which of course, in turn, leads to happiness.

Being part of a pack, a gang, a team, a squad, a community, helps solidify your foundations for a happy life. Human connection creates love, positive revolutions, multiplied power and a web of courage and strength. What a joy it is to stumble across wonderful beings that understand you and LOVE you, and what a blessing it is to be able to love and understand others in this life, too.

Loneliness is a huge problem on this planet – it causes so much heartache and desperation. No one should have to feel lonely; every one of us deserves to have that unbreakable forcefield of friendship and love around them. If you feel lonely reach out for support, it could be nearer than you think. If you see someone that seems lonely, open your world up to them and help them see how important that connection can be.

I have always been on the lookout for a gang. I love the sensation of belonging, where inhibitions and barriers dissipate in seconds as you all revert to your own pack lingo and stories. I'm extremely fortunate to have a very tight-knit and beautiful friendship with five girls I went to school with. We grew up in the same suburban town, all went on to have very different careers, and now most of us have kids, so are experiencing motherhood together, too.

Whatever is going on in our lives, or however many months it has been since we have all sat nattering together, we click back into our patterns and habits and laugh about old times with the warmth of nearly thirty years of friendship behind us. This is a group of individuals that I constantly feel lucky to have in my life. No matter how lost I feel, I know I belong in this team of women. In your own moments of feeling lost or down, draw on your own team and lean in to them; depend on them and let them flex their friendship muscles.

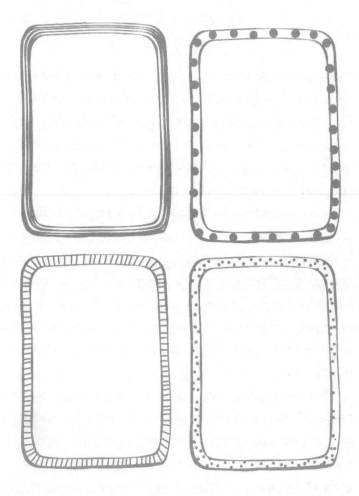

We all have packs and groups we fit into in life. It could be mates, family, work colleagues. A gang that you feel **proud** to be part of. Write down any packs you feel you belong in and what you can turn to them for, whether that's **laughter, understanding** or **comfort**, and know when times are tough you can gain strength from these people in your life.

PART OF A MOVEMENT

New packs are equally as exciting and important in life. Some friendships of mine have been short-lived connections that worked at a particular period in my life, others are structurally integral to keeping me in a happy place. Some of these collectives are not personal relationships, but instead are a movement I fit into. We can all feel part of something by expressing our own passions and attracting the right people. You might love football, so have a gang of fellow footie fans you feel a sense of belonging with. You may love a certain band and find some like-minded souls who dance in tune with you. We all fall into a wave of thinking with others at some point in our lives, whether consciously or not.

In my early twenties I started working in the music industry via my TV and radio work and loved it. This was a new culture to be submerged in, and I felt part of an extended gang of people who all loved watching live music and hearing anything that made the hairs on the back of their necks stand on end. I felt as if the whole music world was moving and breathing as one, and I would constantly bump into the same faces at different shows and work events. There was a constant, exciting dialogue that you could pick up at any point with any person. This sort of pack didn't necessarily provide me with a deep and nourishing support network, but I had the feeling of belonging. I still do.

POCKETS OF PEOPLE

I have found that as you get older your friendship circles naturally tend to shrink as you know who truly brings you that freeing joy. I used to have house parties full of people I knew, kind of knew and really didn't know at all. That was all part of the fun and thrill of it all; having a great time with an eclectic mix of strangers who had a loose common thread of sort-of knowing me. What could go wrong? Well, many light fixtures and loo seats were accidentally broken, but it was fun and again I felt like I was with a group of people that wanted to have a great time.

Now, I have different categories of packs. Aside from my old school chums, I'm lucky enough to have a diamond-strength pack called 'My Family'. My husband and kids are the ultimate gang – they bring me just the right amount of joy, support, laughter, troubles and irritation to keep me topped up with love and learning at the same time. I have the Cottons and the Woods, who are an eclectic mix of characters and personalities. Being part of these two gangs makes me feel very safe.

I also have a wonderful new gaggle of people I adore and have stumbled across slightly later in life, all of whom I can be 100 per cent myself with, relaxing into familiar conversation. I will crowd my dining room table with these extraordinary people, who all come from different walks of life, and chat it out. This is one of my favourite things to do. In these moments I feel anything could happen: an idea could spring up and bounce around the room; a piece of advice could settle a worry or doubt, sending instant calm through the air; a story could be told which pushes out rumbles of laughter from the pits of our bellies. Conversation sparks, love is circulating and energies change all around.

I feel exceptionally lucky to have these pockets of people that give me a feeling of belonging. That doesn't mean everyone gets on all of the time, but it means when we're not, we all know it'll be okay in the end anyway. You have a shorthand and a backstory, so problems can be worked through as a greater love is supporting you all.

THE SMILE CHART

Keep a record today of every time you smile by writing what made you happy on the faces. KEEP SMILING! It's such a beautiful sight for others to see and also a great way of getting your brain to catch up with what's going on physically!

A PROBLEM SHARED IS
A PROBLEM HALVED

Having good friends is one of the simplest yet most powerful gifts we can experience. Give me coffee with a great mate over a new pair of shoes any day. When you are with someone who understands and truly knows you, it gives you the privilege to open up and talk, and also allows you to properly listen, offering a chance to learn. You have the opportunity to be passionate and enthusiastic, knowing that what you say won't be met with any judgement. It gives you the breathing space to talk about concerns that have been magnified by time and mental solitude. When I have a problem or a worry I have certain go-to friends that I know will instantly help ease that acute brain pain. I will share a story or concern I've had festering for days, and once the words have tumbled out of my mouth in an anxious flurry, I'll already feel like the problem is much, much smaller. Having that human connection and another mind on the case is the best tonic out there.

Storing worries up inside is so pointless. Sometimes we think we have to be tough and deal with situations on our own. Other times we may feel too ashamed or too scared to say the words out loud. Shame is a dangerous feeling that blocks us from being able to share. It's debilitating and unnecessary. A great friend will sit and listen to your story and put that fire of shame out in a single moment; they will squash that suffocating feeling and lighten your load.

I have, time and time again, experienced the power of this transaction, where two humans connect and change the direction of the wind. Allowing another to hear your story might change your perspective and the journey of your thoughts. This can be a game changer. Talk, talk, talk and always listen. Both will lead you to clarity and understanding that is waiting to unfold.

THE PRIVILEGE OF PAYING IT FORWARD

I feel massively privileged to have friends who have come to me needing advice and help. I feel honoured that they feel relaxed enough with me that they can open up and be vulnerable, as they know I won't judge them. Helping a friend in need is a joy and often one of the most feel-good transactions you can be part of. That's the selfish part of being selfless! You do something for another without expecting any gain, but ultimately it'll make you feel so good simultaneously.

Helping a stranger has the same heart-filling qualities, but with an extra buzz attached. You feel like you've broken an unspoken rule, or stepped out of your own life for a few moments. It's a chance for you to be vulnerable by offering your own strengths to another without knowing how that gesture will be met. You could pay for a stranger's coffee, help someone who has broken down at the side of the road, or even just hold the door open for someone, with a smile. You're sending out ripples of happiness and it's boomeranging straight back to you, too. What's not to love?!

LEARN FROM YOUR FRIENDS

When we feel down it is easy to shut off, curl into a ball and hide from the world and others around you. You sever the ties that hold you close to your loved ones and go it alone as it's too painful to include others in your downward spiral. I do this at times. Sometimes, I have to let myself pass through this negative patch naturally and know that it will subside in time. When the storm has settled I can then reach out for that much-needed help and re-connect once again.

As you are now aware, I am useless at relaxing. It doesn't come naturally to me as I feel like I need to be constantly achieving, even on the smallest level. Just this week, I was with my friend, Bonny, who is brilliantly wise and open. Now in her seventies, she has had a curious life of travelling, loving and being, and I learn so much from her when we sit and chat. She is the master of stillness and when we are together she is the yin to my yang. She could sense I was feeling on edge, as I was worrying about the kids and hadn't managed to switch off from the day. She physically moved my body into a relaxed position on the sofa and stretched my legs out in front of me. She said, in her low, gravelly, knowing voice 'RELAAAAAX', and I instantly felt the concerns evaporate. My muscles loosened and I hooked into her way of thinking and being for the evening. We sat and talked about life and love, and she took me into a space I wouldn't have even bothered visiting without her presence; a much needed space where I let the adrenalin dissipate and my mind stop whirring. Our connection allowed me to have this moment and to remember the importance of just BEING. Learning from friends and seeing the world from their point of view, if only for a moment, could be the change you need.

OPEN YOUR MIND

We may also isolate ourselves from others at times to avoid taking a closer look at ourselves. If we have convinced ourselves of certain theories that aid us in getting what we think we want or need, it is hard to hear other opinions if they differ from our own. Perhaps you believe you only amount to what you achieve, so are constantly working yourself into the ground. Friends and those that love you may try to persuade you there's another way but listening to them and having that connection means you have to change your whole set-up. It seems easier to shut off and carry on just as you are.

Maybe you're in a toxic relationship but are too scared to leave. Your pack around you whisper softly that you might be better off parting ways but you can't hear their words as it's too hard to acknowledge. Cutting yourself off from those who love you is easier than making that huge change in life. We have all done this at some point, to protect ourselves from what we know is true deep down.

Listening to those around you doesn't mean you have to do what everyone else thinks you should do all the time, but if you're open and willing to do so then this will help you feel like you're not in it alone, and may show you a happier path.

MAGIC CONNECTIONS

How lucky we are as humans to experience love; that magic and energy that comes when you meet another in life who you spark with. You may have experienced this when you met your partner in life, a friend or your own child. The air around you is full of frenetic crackles that can't be seen but are felt in every cell of your body, a magic that weaves its way into every corner of your being and redirects your path in life.

Human connections have shaped who I am, the choices I make, and how I see the world. Even if everything else around me seems to be falling apart, I can take stock and feel gratitude for those people in my life who continuously bring me the magic.

Never underestimate human touch, kind words and small gestures. Connect with others, remember we are all in it together. and share what you need to, when you need to.

Summary

DEPEND ON YOUR PACK.

Whoever they are, laugh with them and lean on them.

PAY IT FORWARD.

Smile at a stranger and share the happiness.

LEARN FROM YOUR FRIENDS.

Listen to their different points of view and see if they will take you on a new path.

WHAT DOES HAPPY **SHARED** LOOK LIKE TO YOU?

Write one word or draw a picture here that sums it up

HAPPY *Heart*

When I fall in love, I fall deep, fast and intensely. It could be with a person, a song, or a place. I get intoxicated and can think of little else. Wonderful! Most era-defining music has been written about love. Films study and depict its heart-pounding magic. People move across continents, lose sleep and can't eat because of it. Love. The untouchable elation born in the heart.

A LOVE OF MY OWN

I met my husband in Ibiza in 2011. That incredibly magical island is one of those places that has my 'LOVE' stamp all over it. It's a place where anything can happen. Meeting Jesse there made it even more special to me, on that balmy June evening.

Love can turn up in many ways, and at varying speeds. It's not always instant, but with my husband it was. We were introduced by mutual friends, spookily on the anniversary of his mum's passing. Time seemed to cease and the loud music playing seemed insignificant. It's hard to describe the feelings that surrounded that night and the following months, where we got to know each other and worked out how we would intertwine in each other's lives, but it was definitely magic: otherworldly feelings took over my whole body and mind. Moments like these make me realise how out of control we are in life, and that that can be a good thing – something can suddenly happen to change your world forever. This magic changed my perspective about everything.

If you've fallen in love you'll know how all-consuming and dreamlike this magic is. You can't see it, touch it, or bottle it. It's simply buzzing in the energy all around, as two people meet and instantly connect in a deep way. I feel incredibly lucky to have experienced this in my lifetime, as it makes me feel so alive and changed the whole story of my life.

Once that initial frantic, urgent and frenetic new love settles, that magic morphs into a new form of love; a steady and comfortable warmth that allows you to feel supported and safe wherever you are. It's still exciting and fun, but the adrenalin expires and leaves you with all the good bits soaked in. I am so grateful that the foundations of my life are now solidified with this kind of love. I feel lucky that I am in a partnership that allows me to make mistakes and show my scars and vulnerabilities, as it's held together by the heart. Out of this love have come our two beautiful babies and my amazing stepchildren.

KIDS

I feel truly blessed that I got to experience being a stepmum before I had my own kids. My stepchildren welcomed me into their lives without judgement or fear and for that I'm eternally grateful. I love them both a lot and adore the fact that my ever-changing life and dynamic is fenced in by such wonderful humans.

I had no idea how it would actually feel to be a mum until my first-born sprung into the world on a snowy February morning.

The love I felt during my long and intense labour was already more overwhelming than I could have imagined. It was the power that got me through the acute surges, which were also a shock! I saw rainbows as the contractions peaked and for the first time noticed how closely linked extreme pain can be to sheer joy. A contraction would climb and climb, then tip over from mind-combusting sensations to white-noise joy. It all felt astounding. Again, there was that magic, that inexplicable energy taking over the show!

I ended up having an epidural after twenty-odd hours of labour, as I wasn't progressing as quickly as I should have been. But, when I first got to hold Rex in my arms and looked into his knowing eyes, I was struck by a wonder and happiness that I hadn't experienced before. It wasn't like the rushing and dizzy love when I first set eyes on my husband, and it wasn't like the love I have for my parents. It was a new shape of love I had no idea existed.

My labour with Honey was a different experience, as I had decided, after a long, drawn-out labour first time round, that I would try hypno-birthing. Through it I experienced even more life-changing feelings. Firstly, I had no idea how powerful my mind could be, working in tandem with my physically exhausted body. They worked together, along with Honey, to create a much swifter and calmer birth. I put zero pressure on myself as I didn't mind how the labour itself went as long as the baby was delivered safely, but I'm so grateful I got to enjoy that powerful experience, again doused in that ethereal magic.

Honey floated up to the surface of the water in the birthing pool with a mop of red hair and a serene glow, and it was love at first sight again. I had no idea there was more love to give, but as soon as I held her in my arms it came crashing out in huge waves. I buzzed for days afterwards and this magical energy whirled around the sleepless nights and stream of visitors, giving me strength I had no idea existed. Once again, that invisible magic has the power to change how you do things and boost your life in unimaginable ways. If you have children of your own, you'll know how fierce that love is: it is a shield that you will use to protect them, to care for them, to learn with them. Even when your kids are pushing boundaries and causing chaos, you deal with it all with an undercurrent of love.

What ten people or things in your life equal pure **love**?

FRIENDSHIP

Meeting a wonderful person and forming a strong bond of friend-ship is another event saturated in love. I feel extremely lucky to have some incredible humans in my life whom I truly love with all my heart. Falling in love with friends is an ecstasy that keeps on giving. Friendships can last a lifetime and just keep getting stronger. Recently, I was at a wedding with my close school friends and we danced and sang and laughed all night. I felt giddy with love by the end of it all. These friends are friends that bear no judgement, and see you in the best light. You are in their hearts always and they are in yours.

FEEL THE LOVE

 So, look around you. How much love can you feel? I can find it in my family and my friends, and I urge you to find it, see it and feel it, too. Don't be complacent and forget its beauty and importance. It's all that really matters amid all the drama we stage around our lives. Watch out for its signs, listen to its voice and hold it lightly, knowing it comes and goes in different forms.

We can't capture love or take it prisoner. We have to let it breathe and run its course naturally. This could be for an eternity, or maybe minutes. If I fall in love with a song I will be tempted to play it on repeat, each time hoping to hear something new, desiring a higher high from its harmonies and soaring chorus at each play. I'll do this until I notice the feelings dulling – the notes feeling less full-bodied and the words not jumping out and attaching to my own story in quite the same way. I've overdone it. I tried to cage that feeling and fast-tracked its exit from my life. We are all capable of doing this with songs, people, jobs, places and ways of thinking. Learning to let things take their natural course is tough, but it's so necessary if we want to truly experience their glory.

LOVE LOSS

Break-ups are shit. Even if your own heart has closed off from your partner and you want out, it's still a tough change that is hard to make. I have been on the receiving end of this rejection far more times than the other way round, and it is soul-wrenching. If you've been in a long-term relationship that comes to an end, you feel lost. Every familiar element of your life looks different and seems distorted. That magic has vanished and left huge holes dotted around your life that you're not sure how to fill. I've dealt with this loss in many different ways over the years and, from my experience, filling those barren chasms in your world with fun is the best way of coping.

I used to go through a period of mourning where I dived straight into a sea of sad songs and lonely nights in ugly pyjamas, but once this became overly isolating I took a step outside my comfort zone and looked for fun. It feels like you're faking it at first, but soon your mind catches up with your smile and you're en route to a happier existence, without that person. This fun could be dancing with friends until your feet hurt. Moving your body and letting off steam to music is so therapeutic. I always find that when you're in a post-relationship headspace, you care far less what others think of you as you feel you have nothing to lose. This is the perfect time to go and dance! Be wild, be your alter ego for the night. Or do something you have always wanted to do but haven't had the guts to. Dye your hair a new colour, go on a trek with a friend to a place you've never been to before. Camp under the stars. Try a new hobby. Just do something that is detached from your past rela-tionship and what that meant to you – something new, inspiring, and exhilarating. Fun can take the place of that love until the magic arrives on your doorstep again.

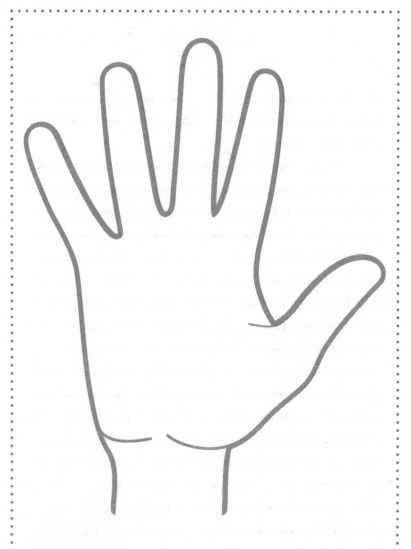

Write a **positive** thing about yourself on each finger. Every time you look down at your own hands or wash them, remember these positives you have committed to. The power of self-love!

When I was twenty-nine I found myself single and lost. I had imagined I would be married with kids at this point so felt like a failure for a long while. Once I had dug myself out of this hole I leaned in to a new frame of mind, accepting that maybe I just wouldn't meet anyone in life. I switched off my hopes to meet someone and found a new rhythm in life that felt good. This is the exact moment I met my husband. Because I had stopped worrying about finding THE ONE and started thinking outside the box, I think I was open to receiving new forms of love in new ways. I had no clue I would meet my husband while I was on a girls' holiday in Ibiza. It was the last thing on my mind. I was happy feeding off the love from my wonderful mates who had arranged the trip. Never give up hope if you haven't yet found your love. Have the confidence that you'll find it or it'll find you, and be open to it arriving in a different form to what you may have in mind.

Losing a relative or friend you love seems to make no sense. Nearly all of us will have lost friends or family members to illness, old age or tragedy and it always feels unjust and mind-boggling. This sort of love-loss void is incomparable and excruciating, as you learn to trek on without these special people around. I'm not sure if anyone knows truly how to deal with this sort of trauma, other than to surround yourself with good people to take care of you. Let yourself feel the sorrow for as long as feels natural to you. Don't rush it or numb it, as it'll come back again at full strength when you're least expecting it. Let the loss digest, and deal with it in the gentlest way possible, with self-love and care. These tragic losses always make you assess your own life and how you live it, which again shows the power of love even when you think it's gone. It lives on, breathes on and weaves into your life in new, unexpected ways.

LOVING AGAIN

When you've been hurt in a relationship, it can be difficult to lean in to love afterwards, as that vulnerability feels too treacherous. Falling in love is one of the most vulnerable things you can do: you are falling head first into someone else's world without knowing which direction it'll spin you in. When you've experienced love-loss after taking such a gamble it's hard to trust again. You create barriers that protect you from what you've been through. You view others with a more judgmental eye and you can't quite visualise it all going well. This is when we get into patterns of behaviour that can be destructive. You don't act from that fiery pit of love but instead act on past trauma and fear. Once you've spotted those patterns and roles you slip into, you can start to unpick them. Leaning in to love is terrifying when you've had your heart broken, but strengthening your own hope, trust and ability to be vulnerable will get you there, and once you do it's so worth it.

DESTRUCTIVE LOVE

How can such a soft, luxurious emotion ever lead you down a negative road?

With a destructive dynamic in play, love can lead you down a lonely path. If you feel you are being leaned on too heavily, are treated badly by someone, or can see how your relationship is changing your life for the worse, it might be time to reassess this love and see if it still fits into your plans. Being in a relationship will always have its ups and downs and will require work and compromise, but if the negatives outweigh the positives, this love might not be worth the fight.

SELF-LOVE

It sounds cheesy and very un-British to be anywhere near self-love, but really it's the guts of it all. If you can truly love and accept yourself and your mistakes, letting in love is much, much easier.

Who doesn't love receiving snail mail that isn't a bill?! Write a loved one a love letter, telling them all the things you love about them. Then cut out this page to post off to them today!

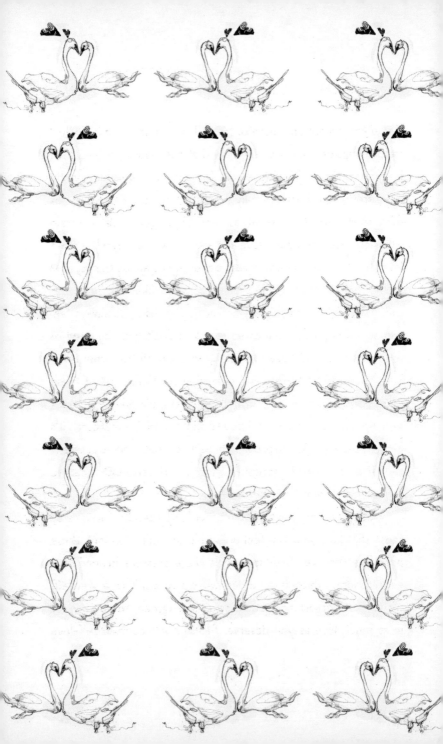

If you can accept and learn to love all your quirks and individual traits alongside your past and how that has made you feel, then it is easy to let someone love you. There is nothing to hide or shy away from, so others can fully embrace you as you are. I'm not quite there with this one yet, as I know I get defensive in certain situations because I don't love and accept parts of myself: I don't love that I get overly enthusiastic and urgent about things, as it makes me feel like a giddy teenager; I don't like to fully accept the fact that I didn't do that brilliantly at school, so always feel paranoid around very educated people; I don't love my need to feel in control and have everything in order all the time; and I long to be more carefree and relaxed about things. All of these (and more) make me act out if they are stimulated in conversation. I pounce like a cat and hiss and shout until I've forgotten it's actually me who has the problem with these traits and no one else. But I'll keep striving to accept how I am and the strengths that are formed because of these personal quirks.

When you don't love yourself much, you tend to push away those that love you. You feel unlovable so can't even look these people in the eye. Their love feels like a pressure heaped with expectations, which is a burden when you don't love yourself. It's such an important foundation to strengthen, so you can let in as much love as you deserve. Please don't confuse self-love with arrogance. When the ego takes over and makes someone think they're invincible there is actually usually a big dose of deep self-love needed. Real self-love is all about acceptance and acting from that place. So love yourself, then let others love you, too.

Love . . . you thrilling, spine tingling, intoxicating, life-changing, awakening feeling. I'm ready for you, always!

Summary

FEEL THE LOVE.

Recognise where it is in your life, notice it and let it wash over you.

DON'T LET LOVE GO.

Draw good memories from those you've lost; they're there with you always.

SELF-LOVE.

The key to it all. Let's strive to love ourselves so everyone else can, too.

WHAT DOES HAPPY **HEART**
LOOK LIKE TO YOU?

Write one word or draw a picture here that sums it up

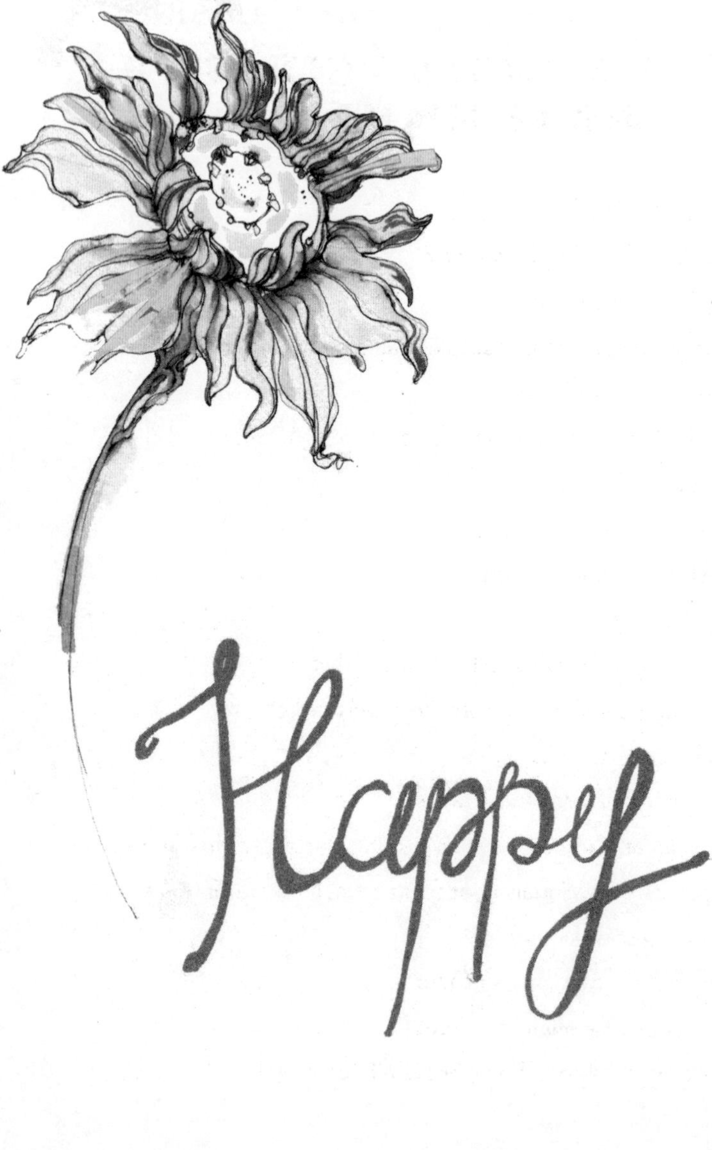
Happy

SOME SMALL THINGS THAT MAKE ME HAPPY . . .

My son's dimples

My daughter's bright red hair

My husband's jokes

Watching my kids and stepkids all play together

The colour light pink

New underwear (doesn't happen enough)

A new cookbook

Vinyl

Mist over my local park

A good coffee

Watching a Disney short called *La Luna*

Getting a parking space at the supermarket

Walking in the rain

Cleaning my kitchen surfaces

Looking at photos from a trip to Ibiza with my girlfriends

A pair of pink sandals I got from a small market in Ibiza

Ibiza in general

The first sip of a gin and tonic

Stepping off a plane into heat

Getting stuck into a new book in bed

Lying on the grass looking at the sky

Stirring cake mixture

Buying people birthday gifts

Dark chocolate, sucked not chewed

Lying in a hammock

Getting under the covers at night

Freshly painted toenails

Hearing the ocean

Garlic in everything

Thinking about the jam and salty butter on brown bread my nan used to give me.

Looking at kitchens on Pinterest

Assembling cakes

Rearranging furniture

Giving stuff to the charity shop

Happiness, you gorgeous warm ray of sunshine. I love it when you spring up out of nowhere and take me by surprise and how you can make clouds part and corners of mouths lift.

I love that you have been there in so many special moments in my life and for that I'm beyond grateful. I love that you still attach yourself to certain memories I can recall in an instant. I have a box stored of these times that seem magical and cinematic to recall.

How lucky I feel to have basked in your rays during these moments.

I know that to truly welcome you into my life I have to work with you daily and not let you get drowned out by life's circus. I have to sink into your arms and then let you go when other important emotions need to pass through. I need to remember that you'll always come back looking for me if my eyes are wide enough and my heart is open. That's a choice I can make daily so I endeavour to keep this firmly in mind.

Thank you for leaving my life at times to allow me to experience your vast contrast. These moments have felt hollow and cold but were true reminders of how sweet life is with you in it. They've also given me insights into other parts of my mind I hadn't previously accessed. Although tough, I can see the value in your disappearance and distance. At times I may have thought I'd lost you for good but now know with clarity that you'll always be nearby, waiting to make a return.

I love how you appear in many different forms and at the oddest of times and will forever look forward to you popping up when my eyes have been diverted the other way. I will always trust in your covert movements and keep my heart open for you. I will then send you off in many different directions for others to share too.

That's the beauty of you, Happiness: you just keep on travelling . . .

HAPPY THANK YOUS

Here's where I get to say those much needed thank yous and truly mean it. I want to start with you. Thank you for seeing this book in a shop or online and thinking that it might add something to your life. That is what I was hoping for, so I'm glad that the cover leapt out at you and sparked interest. I was nervous about writing this book so the fact that you decided to give it a read means a lot to me. I hope this book has helped you to take a look at the happiness in your life and how best you can access it. THANK YOU.

A gargantuan thank you to Amanda and Emily at Orion who once again let me muse, ponder and type freely, with such beautiful guidance and reassurance in moments of apprehension. Your support and belief in the project gave it sturdy roots to grow from and for that I'm very grateful.

Thanks to Rowan at Furniss Lawton for keeping me on track with this in-depth project and for encouraging me when needed. Thanks to Rachel, Sarah, Claire and Mary at James Grant. My very own golden girls who constantly cheerlead me from the side/give me pep talks/tell me to shut up. Your honesty, love and friendship means the world to me. True sisterhood.

One human who needs a massive dollop of thanks is my darling husband, who has watched me sit typing at a laptop for almost a year. You have replenished me with hot tea and the odd shoulder massage and have been an incredible sounding board for my general worries and concerns. You also helped me stagger through my dark patch with deep love wrapped in a layer of calm. Thank you Jesse. Soulmate stuff!

Thank you to my children and stepchildren for simply being YOU. Each of you teach me so much about life and love every day and that has helped fuel this writing process on a deeper level. I love you.

Thank you to all of my wonderful family and friends who have given me advice and love over the years. Your words and wisdom have made such an impact on my life and these pages.

Thanks Jessie May for providing such beautiful illustrations for the book to go alongside my own. Your friendship and understanding of this subject meant you were the perfect artist for the job!

Thank you to Zephyr for teaching me the ways of yoga and how it can enhance your life. I adore your classes and have drawn so much from your deep understanding of life and love. Thank you for supplying such wonderful yoga sequences for this book.

Gerad AKA Gezza, I'm so grateful for your friendship and grounding words. Your theories and kind words always get me thinking outside the box. You have taught me so much over the years so I'm over the moon you could contribute to *Happy*, too.

Tom Fletcher. I think one of the reasons I've been able to be so honest in this book, is due to witnessing your own, open approach to life. Thanks for sharing once again, in my book.

Thank you Hollie De Cruz for conjuring up such a beautiful mediation. I can almost hear your calming tones float off the pages!

Thanks, Craig David. Your positivity and optimism have always inspired me, so thanks for taking the time to chat as part of this project.

Thanks Kris for being a great mate, inspiring me and thousands of others, and for letting me design the tattoo you now proudly wear on your chest. You rock!

Thank you Liam Arthur for snapping the photos for the book! Fun music-filled shoots always equal happiness.

Thank you Ben Gardiner for getting the design of this book spot on. I feel lucky I got to work with this wonderful group of people.

Uncle Hadyn, thank you. I'm so glad we recently reconnected and have started such a wonderful flow of communication over email. Your news always brightens my week. Thank you for telling your story here, too.

Thanks and many happy times to you all.

F x